A HANDBOOK OF ECONOMIC INDICATORS

Second Edition

Every day brings new reports and statistics on the economy, but most of us find it difficult to fit these indicators together to form a coherent picture. This book should help non-economists, whether journalists, managers, students, or investors, to do just that.

Nine chapters explain in straightforward terms the role of households, businesses, governments, and foreign interests in the economy, and how their economic activities are measured. The author clearly describes the 'how' and 'why' of monetary and fiscal policies and their interactions. One chapter explains how wages and employment are determined.

The last two chapters look at the major Canadian and U.S. economic indicators, such as the consumer price index, housing starts, and employment data. What information do they contain? When are they released? What website can they be found at? How reliable are they? What is their significance? The author helps the reader weigh the information in the indicators in order to anticipate economic developments.

For the businessperson who needs to understand the economy's impact on the 'bottom line,' for the student who wants to bridge the gap between theory and the 'real world,' for the individual who wants to make better investment decisions, this handbook provides clear, concise guidance.

JOHN GRANT is adjunct professor in the Department of Business Economics in the Joseph L. Rotman School of Management, University of Toronto. He was for over two decades chief economist for a leading Canadian investment dealer.

JOHN GRANT

A Handbook of Economic Indicators

Second Edition

UNIVERSITY OF TORONTO PRESS
Toronto Buffalo London

© University of Toronto Press Incorporated 1999
Toronto Buffalo London
Printed in Canada

ISBN 0-8020-0878-X (cloth)
ISBN 0-8020-7863-X (paper)

Printed on acid-free paper

Canadian Cataloguing in Publication Data

Grant, John
 A handbook of economic indicators

 2nd ed.
 Includes bibliographical references
 ISBN 0-8020-0878-X (bound)   ISBN 0-8020-7863-X (pbk.)

 1. Economic forecasting – Canada.   2. Canada – Economic
 conditions – 1991– .*   3. Economic forecasting – United States.
 4. United States – Economic conditions – 1981–   .   6. Economic
 indicators – Canada.   7. Economic indicators – United States.
 I. Title.

 HB3730.G73 1999   330.971'.064   C98-932772-8

University of Toronto Press acknowledges the support to its publishing program of the
Canada Council for the Arts and the Ontario Arts Council.

Contents

Acknowledgments

The first edition of this book, published in 1992, drew heavily on my experience as chief economist at Wood Gundy and emphasized the role of economic indicators in framing an overview of the economic outlook. Since that book appeared, I have had the benefit of teaching macro-economics to students in the Executive MBA and the Master of Management and Professional Accounting programs at the University of Toronto, and this experience made it clear to me that there is a need for a brief overview of the macro-economic framework into which the indicators can fit.

There are many excellent texts in macro-economics. However, most of them arguably provide more information and depth on the subject than the typical manager wishes to absorb. The reader knows better than I whether this book goes too far or not far enough; my own hope is that it will encourage many readers to go deeper into the subject, because it will quickly become clear that the chapter discussions are really simply an introduction to the topics that they raise.

Since the first edition the Internet has grown to become the premier means of communication, in this as in so many other fields. The last two chapters discuss the Canadian and U.S. indicators individually and now provide web addresses where they can be found, and a number of websites that provide remarkable resources for economists and would-be scenario builders.

I am most grateful to officials at Statistics Canada and the Bank of Canada who took time to provide comments as the book was prepared. I also thank the University of Toronto Press, and my students, for encouraging me to deal with the challenge of this expanded second edition. However, none of them can be charged with responsibility for the errors that can undoubtedly be found here.

John Grant
August 1998

Abbreviations

BCN	Bureau of the Census, U.S. Department of Commerce
BCR	*Bank of Canada Review* (quarterly)
BEA	Bureau of Economic Analysis, U.S. Department of Commerce
BLS	Bureau of Labor Statistics, U.S. Department of Labor
BOP	Balance of Payments
CANSIM	Statistics Canada's computer-readable database
CCA	capital consumption allowances
CMHC	Canada Mortgage and Housing Corporation
CPA	Canadian Payments Association
CPI	consumer price index
ECI	Employment Cost Index (U.S.)
FFA	Financial Flow Accounts
FRB	board of governors of the Federal Reserve System, Washington, DC
GDE	gross domestic expenditure at market prices
GDP	gross domestic product at market prices
GDPFC	gross domestic product at factor cost
GNE	gross national expenditure at market prices
GNP	gross national product at market prices
IMF	International Monetary Fund, Washington, DC
IOA	Input–Output Accounts
IPPI	Industrial Product Price Index (Canada)
IVA	inventory valuation adjustment
LFS	Labour Force Survey (Canada)
NAICS	North American Industry Classification System
NBSA	National Balance Sheet Accounts
NDI	net domestic income
NEFA	National Economic and Financial Accounts (Canada)

NIEA	National Income and Expenditure Accounts (Canada)
NIPA	National Income and Product Accounts (U.S.)
NSA	not seasonally adjusted
PDI	personal disposable income
PEA	Provincial Economic Accounts
PPI	Producer Price Index (U.S.)
RMPI	Raw Materials Price Index (Canada)
SA	seasonally adjusted
SAAR	seasonally adjusted at annual rates
SIC	Standard Industrial Classification (precursor of NAICS)
SNA	system of national accounts

A HANDBOOK OF ECONOMIC INDICATORS

Introduction

This book introduces you to the way the Canadian economy works and suggests a way to make sense of the major economic indicators that are published from day to day. I do not assume that you have prior formal training in economics or accounting. Whereas textbooks concentrate on theory, this book has a different aim: to strengthen your intuition about what is going on out there, so that you can make your business (and for that matter household) decisions more confidently and effectively.

Statistics Canada ('StatsCan'), the U.S. Department of Commerce, and other agencies publish many economic indicators each day. This book explains how you can integrate them into a perspective of your own. In the first place, you need to understand what the names mean – what is referred to when 'housing starts went up' or when 'GDP went down.' Second, you need to know how the indicators fit together. Third, you need to grasp what drives the economic decisions taken by the various sectors of the economy. And finally, you need to understand what central banks such as the Bank of Canada and the U.S. Federal Reserve Board (the 'Fed') do, because they, in effect, are the managers of the show.

Even for the experts, the economy can be hard to read. Individuals, households, enterprises, and governments around the world make billions of economic decisions every day, and only a few are reported on quickly. Even the best-informed forecasters have to rely partly on intuition to anticipate what is likely to happen next. However, the situation is not as bad as it may sound. Though some claim that the economy is inherently chaotic, there are strong stabilizing forces at work; and there is a structure – the system of national accounts (SNA) – that helps us to organize our thinking. That is where we start.

The SNA organizes a country's economic decision-makers into four sectors: households, enterprises, governments, and non-residents. There is some overlap (householders operate small businesses, for example), but the SNA reports on what each sector is doing, and this allows us to make judgments about their behaviour and pull them together into a general view.

The Central Theme: The Circular Flow

One central image dominates macro-economics[1] – the 'circular flow' (the subject of chapter 1). Each sector buys goods and services, and the producers earn income from producing them. The sectors' incomes become the basis for a new round of spending – and so it goes, round and round. In this book I examine the three main sectors in the Canadian economy – households (chapter 2), enterprises (chapter 3), and governments (chapter 4). The total of goods and services produced within the borders of the country during a quarter or a year is called the gross domestic product (GDP); macro-economics is largely about how GDP is determined.

Can we meaningfully speak of economic decisions being made by a sector, as opposed to the individual entities within it? Yes, if we see it as a useful fiction. Households' aggregate consumption can actually be pretty well explained by relating it to aggregate household income. More detailed information on the characteristics and expectations of individual households would permit a better explanation, but useful predictions can be made without it.

Wealth versus Income

In common speech, when we speak of someone's wealth, we sometimes mistakenly mean the size of his or her income. Income from various sources – earnings from a job, old age pensions, gifts from relatives, interest from bonds – can be thought of as a set of flows, taking place at various rates over time. 'Wealth' more properly refers to a stock of assets, measured at a particular point of time. (Liabilities are, in effect, negative assets.) Flows of purchases of goods and services, and lending and borrowing flows as well, represent decisions by households, enterprises, and governments to manage their wealth – their portfolios of assets and liabilities.

So, while wealth can generate income, and income can be used to accumulate wealth, they are not the same thing. This distinction between stocks and flows is generally highly important in macro-economics.

---

1 Macro-economics, as opposed to micro-economics, studies aggregated economic behaviour – for example, it tries to explain the consumption of Canadians as a whole, rather than the consumption decisions of individual entities.

Expectations

Expectations about the future are also important in macro-economics. They determine the value of assets such as bonds, shares, houses, even machines. Anything that is wanted because of the services or income that it can provide in the future has its value set by expectations. Discussions about the economy often involve expectations – newspapers may refer, for instance, to the 'expected inflation rate.' Whose expectation? and how formed? – we need to grapple with such questions in coming to understand financial markets, investment, economic growth, and indeed all forecasting issues.

The Central Bank

Very special attention needs to be paid to the central bank (in Canada, the Bank of Canada) (see chapters 5 and 7). Most people think that central banks have a simple mandate — to keep inflation within a certain range. This is true, but that task actually involves managing the whole economy. Modern central banks are not well understood by the public in general but are arguably the most important actors in the macro-economic drama. Despite their role, central banks are more or less independent of political influence from day to day. It is vital to understand how they operate and why.

Fiscal Policy and Management of Public Debt

While the central bank's role is critical, governments' other economic activities are also significant: how much they spend, how much they tax, how much social support they provide. These 'fiscal policy' decisions have a major influence on private decisions as well. And there are very sizeable macro-economic implications. For example, raising income tax rates tends to reduce the amount of private income available for spending, which tends to lead to reduced consumption; as people spend less, they create less income for others, and so spending falls even further. Not only that, but, since income taxes are usually levied as a percentage of income, tax revenues themselves may drop even though the rates have risen.

In recent decades, at least until very recently, Canadian federal and provincial governments have tended to raise less tax revenue than they needed to cover their outlays. As a result, they have run successive annual deficits, which have accumulated into a huge stock of public debt. Debt management and reduction have now become a central focus of fiscal policy, a topic that I explore in chapter 9.

In the 1980s, it could be said that central banks and governments tended to act unharmoniously. When the Bank of Canada attempted to reduce inflation by slowing the economy, governments failed to cope effectively. Tax revenues dropped, and Unemployment Insurance (now Employment Insurance) benefits and social support payments rose because of events in the labour market (chapter 8), worsening their financial position dramatically. In the 1990s, coordination has become more satisfactory, and I explore how.

International Economic Relationships

Transactions with non-residents, and the resulting changes in cross-border claims, are classified in the 'non-resident sector' of the SNA. Canadians' assets abroad are 'claims upon non-residents'; non-residents' claims on Canadians are Canada's foreign liabilities. When one exports goods and services to other countries, one acquires claims on them, unless they have paid for these in advance. These days, however, most international claims arise not from exports and imports of goods and services but from decisions by investors, such as managers of mutual funds, to diversify their portfolios into foreign financial assets. In any case, almost all transactions across borders usually involve two parts: first, the exchange of one currency for another, then use of that currency to buy goods and services or financial assets in the foreign market. Currency exchange rates play a crucial role in Canada's economy, and I explore that subject starting in chapter 6.

Short-Term versus Long-Term Issues

In order to keep this book manageable in size, I do not deal with a number of longer-term issues. Demographics, for instance – the study of population – becomes increasingly relevant the further into the future we peer. And investment – the acquisition of machinery and structures – cannot be understood fully in a short-term context. Intergenerational issues, including the question of what we bequeath to our heirs, are a legitimate concern of macro-economics that we cannot deal with here. This book concentrates on how the economy evolves from quarter to quarter and from year to year.

The Role of Economic Indicators in Forecasting

In most chapters, a brief final section suggests which of the economic indicators are likely to be most helpful in assessing the subject matter of that chapter, with indicators analysed in chapter 11 or 12 rendered in bold face.

Chapter 10 outlines how to use the indicators, and chapters 11 and 12 describe the key Canadian and U.S. economic indicators one by one and indicate how they can help you fit together a coherent picture of the economy. There is a huge army of analysts who avidly anticipate these indicators, construct forecasts and projections around them, and broadcast opinions to all who will listen or pay. But with the insights gained from this book and, even better, from a good course in macro-economics, you can use the indicators yourself and construct your own viewpoint on where the economy is going.

It needs to be said that the indicators do not mean much on their own. Many of them are measured imperfectly; they may be subject to significant revision; and in general, they make sense only by contributing to a larger picture. Though professional forecasters often use complex economic models, they too peer through fog. But when you have an organized conception in your mind of what may lie ahead, the indicators help you to improve that conception; that is the contribution they can make.

1

The Circular Flow

Economic forecasters try to predict human behaviour – but not all of it. Their scope is limited to behaviour that manipulates assets and liabilities. Whatever people do that influences the value of their assets and liabilities is a valid concern for an economist.

Let us start by defining an economic decision: it is a decision that alters one's portfolio of assets and liabilities. It can be implemented by buying, selling, lending, or borrowing – or even by doing nothing. Economic decisions are taken by transactors, who may be individuals, households, small businesses, institutions, corporations, or governments; we may want to identify them as residents or non-residents of the country as well.

At a given point in time, a transactor has a stock of assets and liabilities. One of the most valuable stocks that an individual has is himself or herself, capable of generating a flow over time of labour services, which can be exchanged for money. If we divide time into periods, we can compare the value of a transactor's stock of an asset at the beginning of a period with its value at the end; typically, the value will have changed. What might have happened to change it? Most often, there has been a flow of purchases or sales (in the case of financial assets or liabilities, the flows are referred to as 'lending' or 'borrowing'). But the value of a stock can also change without any flows taking place – for example, as a result of a change in its price. Also, some stocks are not altered by their flows – for example, the value of an individual, as a worker, is not diminished by his or her performing work. Consuming something is a special flow. It is neither a purchase nor a sale, but it may diminish the value of the asset that remains. (If you consume just the services of the asset – if you use a comb, for example – its value may not be reduced!) To put yourself in a forecaster's mind, you have to think about events in the economy as reflecting a multitude of decisions about stocks and flows.

Published economic indicators are usually based on samples or censuses of selected stocks or flows – for example, the flow of purchases of new homes in a given month, or the stock of individuals' credit-card liabilities at a point of time. In some cases the indicators are precise and accurate, but these qualities may have to be traded off against timeliness. The last two chapters of the book discuss the major Canadian and U.S. indicators and comment on their reliability.

Even a perfectly accurate indicator is just a piece of a big jigsaw puzzle. One needs to know where to fit it in and how important it is. This book will not make you an economist, but in it I try to sketch the structure of the economy in enough detail to show how things fit together.

Let us classify the ways in which a particular transactor can change the value of an asset or liability that he or she owns (or owes) during a period of time:

- purchase or sale (a flow)
- lending or borrowing (purchase of a financial asset or creation of a liability) (a flow)
- consuming the asset or its services, which may or may not reduce its remaining value (a flow)
- a change in market price (not a flow)
- passage of time (as when a financial asset becomes a shorter-term instrument or a physical asset deteriorates with age) (not a flow)

Consider the situation of a transactor at the beginning of a period. We describe it by listing assets and liabilities, in volume and value (for example, two cars, worth $30,000). And we may want to distinguish among cost value (what was paid for the asset), book value (how it is carried in the transactor's accounts), and market value (what could be obtained for it in the market-place now).

But the transactor's situation has not yet been fully described. He or she is also the subject of certain contracts, which specify that certain flows will take place in the current or future periods. Usually, for an individual, the most important such contract is a job, which is a commitment to trade a flow of labour services for a wage or salary. There may also be a mortgage, a bank loan, a pension entitlement, and so on. As the contracted flows take place, they change the individual's portfolio of assets and liabilities. For example, receipt of a pay cheque will, in the first instance, add to one's bank deposit. The transactor will have to decide, in the context of start-of-period stocks and the contractual flows for the period, what other flows to undertake in order to end up with the best-structured portfolio at the end of the period.

Flow decisions can thus be alternatively described as stock-managing or portfolio-rebalancing decisions. Remember that the value of the portfolio will typically be changing during a period, even without intervention. A transactor has to take many things into account in deciding what flows to undertake. Generally, economists assume that transactors act in such a way as to maximize the sum of (a) their consumption in this period and (b) the expected end-of-period value of their portfolios – subject to the constraints mentioned above. (An alternative, more comprehensive model of behaviour assumes that transactors think many periods ahead and that they are trying to maximize the net present value of the stream of expected flows from their expected future assets and liabilities. Such a model can account for transactions that have no apparent payoff in the current period, such as getting an education.)

What distinguishes a financial asset from a physical one? First, one transactor's financial asset is often another's liability. If aggregated, they would cancel each other out. (However, some financial assets, such as common shares and real estate deeds, are titles to ownership in existing physical assets and therefore do not cancel out.) Second, financial assets typically consist of contractual promises to pay certain amounts at certain times in the future. Various conditions may apply: the amount may be contingent on various events, present or future; times of payments may be unspecified or contingent; the currency of payment may or may not be the local currency; the financial asset may be transferable or not; and/or the likelihood of receiving payments may be regarded as uncertain. All these elements enter into the price or value of financial assets, which therefore tend to be volatile.

Aggregation

I have described above the considerations affecting decisions by transactors. These considerations are the subject of micro-economic theory. In contrast, macro-economics deals with relationships between aggregates. For example, it may explain the consumption flows of all Canadians added together by reference to the sum of their incomes. But when we aggregate in this way we cannot talk of optimizing behaviour as we could for individual transactors. Therefore forecasters – practitioners of macro-economics – are often on shaky ground when they say that something will happen for such and such a reason. Fortunately, as a matter of empirical fact, there are strong associations between one flow and another at the aggregate level. Macro-theory has built up a large body of knowledge about how aggregate stocks and flows tend to behave. None the less, a good understanding of macro-economic aggregates does depend on insights into how and why portfolio decisions take place at the transactor level.

Expectations

Individuals act according to their constraints (their start-of-period stocks and the contracts into which they have entered) but also according to their expectations. Economists have spent a great deal of effort in trying to understand how expectations are formed and how they influence decisions. Expectations are perhaps particularly important in financial markets, because prices of securities generally represent the present value of streams of expected future payments.

In recent years, improvements in information technology have encouraged transactors in many countries to broaden and diversify their portfolios by acquiring holdings of foreign, as well as domestic, financial assets. Reflecting this trend, there is a tremendous flow of funds into and out of Canada every day. As a result, Canadian interest rates and share prices are increasingly influenced by expectations formed abroad, in the context of portfolio considerations that can be very different from those influencing Canadian investors or borrowers.

Also, each transactor can form expectations over an infinite number of horizons. A decision to buy bonds or common shares may reflect a view on their prices in ten minutes, a month, or a year. The market price of a financial asset thus is inherently difficult to explain (unless it is set administratively, like a chartered bank's prime lending rate), since it reflects the expectations of many different transactors (and, for that matter, non-transactors, who may have bought or sold but choose not to do so) over many horizons. As time passes and new information becomes available, expectations change, spurring transactors to trade assets until their prices reflect the new situation. But some individuals act quickly, and others only after deliberation. The financial market forecaster's problem is partly to predict what the new information will be and partly to intuit how securities prices will change as transactors respond to that information.

Obviously the problem is complex!

As new jigsaw pieces (the economic indicators) keep arriving, the forecaster must fit them into place, but his or her real work is to stand back and grasp the emerging pattern. The indicators often sacrifice accuracy to timeliness, especially at their first release. A good grasp of theory, and familiarity with the history of the economy, are thus essential. Professional forecasters carry around a mental picture of the future, which they continually revise in the light of the changing information they receive.

At this point it should be clear that we need to look at some structure. Is there a standard framework into which one can place the indicators?

The System of National Accounts

Fortunately, the answer is yes. The structure that Statistics Canada and similar agencies in other countries use to report on what is happening in their economies is the system of national accounts, or SNA, which was developed in the 1940s. It concentrates on market-valued activities; for example, it does not measure unpaid household work and does not recognize 'free' environmental resources as part of society's wealth. These shortcomings and others have generated considerable frustration and various efforts to recognize and measure these concepts. However, in its own terms, as a structure that is meant to measure and account for market-based economic activity, the SNA is sophisticated and extremely useful.

The SNA aggregates the transactors in the economy into four sectors: households (persons and unincorporated businesses), corporate enterprises (subdivided into private and public, financial and non-financial), governments (federal, provincial, and local), and non-residents.

Chart 1 illustrates how the four sectors participate in the circular flow of expenditure and income that 'makes the world go around.' In the chart, the flow of expenditures goes counterclockwise around the circle; the goods and services being purchased flow in the opposite direction. The number located beside each item represents its size, in millions of dollars, in 1997. Column 1 in Table 1 organizes the same figures as they are presented in the SNA (with two additional columns, one comparing the values of the expenditure flows to the values that they would have had if they were still valued at 1992 prices, and the other showing the ratio of prices in 1997 to those in 1992; I explain these items below).

Let us enter the circle at the right hand side of the 'equator.' Moving upward and towards the left, we collect together a number of expenditure items: namely, consumption, private gross investment, government capital and current outlays on goods and services, and exports of goods and services, and we subtract imports of goods and services. The sum of these items is gross domestic expenditure (GDE) at market prices, defined as the total of all outlays on unduplicated goods and services, produced in the current quarter within the borders of the country. We must subtract imports, because, while they form part of consumption and so on, they are not produced within Canada's borders.

Why 'unduplicated'? ... to avoid double counting. A dress contains cloth, which contains fibre, which contains chemicals, and so on. The value of the dress purchased by the consumer is sufficient to record, because it contains all the value added at every stage.

Chart 1. The circular flow in the Canadian economy, 1997 (figures in $million; some flows omitted for clarity)

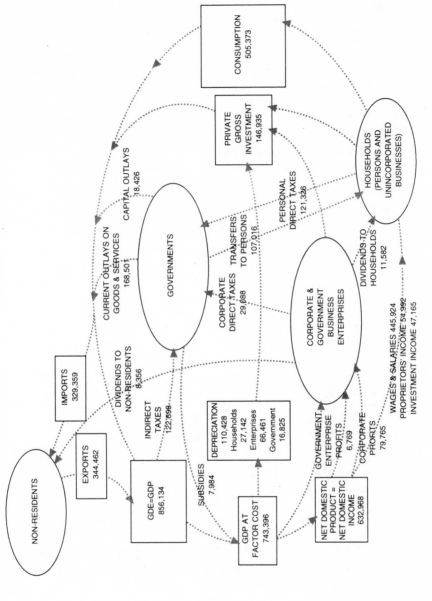

TABLE 1
Canada's circular flow, 1997

	A $million (current)	B $million (1992 dollars)	(A/B) Price level
Personal expenditure on consumer goods and services	505,373	469,282	1.077
+ Net government current expenditure on goods and services	168,501	163,019	1.034
+ Government gross fixed capital formation	18,241	17,760	1.027
+ Business gross fixed capital formation	140,325	132,135	1.062
+ Value of change in government and business inventories	6,615	6,196	1.068
+ Exports of goods and services	344,462	297,985	1.156
− Imports of goods and services	329,359	289,068	1.139
+ Statistical discrepancy	1,976	1,833	
= Gross domestic expenditure at market prices	856,134	799,142	1.071
Wages, salaries, and supplementary labour income	445,924		
+ Corporation profits before taxes	79,765		
+ Government business enterprise profits before taxes	6,769		
+ Interest and miscellaneous investment income	47,165		
+ Net income of unincorporated business, including rent	54,992		
+ Inventory valuation adjustment	−1,647		
= Net domestic income at factor cost	632,968		
+ Capital consumption allowances	110,428		
= Gross domestic product at factor cost	743,396		
+ Indirect taxes less subsidies	114,714		
+ Statistical discrepancy	−1,976		
= Gross domestic product at market prices	856,134		

Source: Statistics Canada, National Income and Expenditure Accounts, #13-001-XPB (fourth quarter 1997), Tables 1, 2, 3.

Note now that GDP, gross domestic product at market prices, has the same value as GDE. This is because they represent exactly the same goods and services; GDE sums them by type of purchase, but GDP sees them from the producer's point of view.[1]

---

1   Actually, there is usually a small difference between the figures as Statistics Canada estimates them; the agency splits the difference on publication, and calls it the 'statistical discrepancy.' See Table 1.

Moving downwards, we reach net domestic product, or net domestic income (NDI). This is the most important income concept in the circular flow: it represents the sum of the incomes earned from producing GDP. But we have skipped over a few items. Let us start at GDP again. Two small flows, just below it, go to and come from government. Indirect taxes (examples are the goods and services tax, provincial sales taxes, and excise taxes) are generally paid by purchasers at the point of sale (and are therefore included in the value of GDE and GDP) but flow to government, not to producers' incomes.[2] By the same token, however, we must add back in subsidies paid to producers by governments. Accounting for these two items takes us from GDP to gross domestic product at factor cost (GDPFC).[3]

We must now subtract one further item from GDPFC in order to arrive at NDI – namely depreciation, grandly titled capital consumption allowances (CCA). Depreciation allowances are the accountant's reminder that machines and structures do not last forever. Having estimated the useful life of an item of capital equipment, a producer is prudent to apportion its acquisition cost over that life and set the proportionate amount aside each period from revenue. The funds do not actually leave the business; they become part of its gross saving and are available to finance the producer's investment outlays at a later stage in the circular flow, as Chart 1 shows; but they must be subtracted from revenue in order to arrive at a prudent determination of income.

NDI is thus the sum of 'factor earnings' – that is, the incomes earned by the contributors to the production process (who provide the 'factors of production'). It consists essentially of four components – wages, salaries, and supplementary labour income (the remuneration of employees); proprietors' income (the incomes of landlords, small business owners, self-employed professionals, and farmers); interest and miscellaneous investment income (the remuneration of lenders for the financing that they have supplied to enterprises);[4] and profits of corporations and government business enterprises.[5] The first three are earned directly by households, but corporate profits are earned by corporate enter-

---

2 Indirect taxes are so called because they are remitted to government not by those who ultimately bear them (the buyers) but by the merchants who collect them.

3 'Factors of production' are the resources that combine to produce the GDP. Some economists categorize them simply as labour and capital; some prefer a more complex classification that may, for example, separate out the contribution of energy.

4 Interest paid by governments is not included here, nor is interest paid on deposits at financial institutions. These are considered to be transfers, not factor income, because they are not payments for contributing to the production of a good or service.

5 There is a fifth item, usually small, called the inventory valuation adjustment (IVA). This adjusts enterprises' reports of profits by removing any write-up or write-down of inventory values that is unrelated to physical additions or subtractions from stock during the period.

prises; however, since households own most corporate shares, they do ultimately receive income from this source as well, in the form of dividends.[6]

What about the role of foreign, as opposed to domestic, shareholders? A great deal of Canadian enterprise over the years has been financed by foreign investors (more recently, Canadians have been acquiring significant interests in foreign enterprises as well). As a result, not all the income from producing Canada's GDP can be attributed to Canadian residents. GDP is the sum of production within Canada's borders, but another measure of Canadian output, called gross national product (GNP), refers to production 'attributable to Canadian residents,' which is not quite the same thing. For instance, if an enterprise produces its goods and services entirely within Canada, all the income earned from it is included in Canada's GDP. But if the enterprise is partly owned in the United States, then some of the income is attributable to Americans and must be subtracted if one is calculating Canada's GNP.

Statistics Canada estimates the difference between GDP and GNP by accounting for the net flow of investment income across the border; if non-residents earn more investment income in Canada than Canadians earn abroad (as is the case), then Canada's GNP is smaller than its GDP (see Table 2). Actually, Canada's GNP has been smaller than its GDP every year as far back as the statistics go, because foreigners have, over the years, provided more financing to the Canadian economy than Canadians have provided to foreign economies.[7]

For the same reason, Canada's NDI, which arises from production within its borders, has been consistently larger than its net national income (NNI), which

TABLE 2
The difference between GDP and GNP ($million), 1997

Gross domestic product at market prices	856,134
+ Investment income earned abroad	23,824
− Investment income earned in Canada by non-residents	−51,752
= Gross national product at market prices	828,206

Source: Statistics Canada, National Income and Expenditure Accounts, #13-001-XPB (fourth quarter 1997), Tables 14, 30.

---

6   The board of directors of a corporation must declare dividends payable in order for them to flow to shareholders.

7   This may finally be changing. As Table 10 below shows, in 1997 direct and portfolio investment abroad by Canadians ($29,326 million) was almost as great as the counterpart inflows to Canada ($32,448 million). If, in future, Canadian lending abroad begins to outpace foreign borrowing, the net flow of investment income will gradually shift in Canada's favour as well.

arises from the domestic and foreign production attributable to Canadian residents. NDI is not the total of incomes received in the economy. A sector may also earn income from transfers, such as gifts that are made to it, or from social insurance benefits, which are not earned from producing goods and services. NDI just totals the factor incomes that are earned in the course of producing GDP.

How Income Is Disposed Of

There are only three ways that a sector can use its income, from whatever sources: first, it can purchase goods and services to be consumed; second, it can make transfers to other sectors, or third, it can save. Saving is the residual category; it is defined as whatever is left over from income after consumption and transfers have been accounted for.

This three-way allocation may seem incomplete. Are there not other outlays that a sector could make besides consumption and transfers? The answer is yes; for example, it can invest (buy capital equipment), and it can lend (acquire financial assets). But the sector can also draw on more than its income to do so! The financing for investment, for lending, and for acquiring pre-existing assets may come from the sector's saving, but it may also come from the sale of pre-existing assets or, very important, from borrowing.

So our chart does not actually show all the major flows in the economy. While it does display all the outlays on goods and services and the incomes earned from producing them, it does not cover the financial flows that are needed to make it all happen – especially borrowing and lending by one sector to another.

We leave the subject here for now and return to it below when I describe the individual sectors. In any case, we have got all the way around the circle of the circular flow, ending with consumption, as we began. To get further into the story, we need to take it sector by sector, starting with households in chapter 2.

The Price Level

All goods or services that enter the market economy are sold at a price. The value of sales in a given period is equal to the volume (the number of physical units) times the price. These apparently innocuous statements conceal a significant issue: the price in terms of what? The price of a good tells the observer how many units of something else it would take to buy a unit of this good. The 'something else' is called the numeraire. The most familiar numeraire is money, since we normally measure values relative to money, as when we say that such-and-such a good has a price of so many dollars. Values measured in money terms are called nominal values, and when we use them, we say that we are measuring in nominal, or sometimes 'current-dollar,' terms.

The price of a commodity typically changes between one period and another. We can index the resulting series by dividing all the prices in the series by the price in one period, called the base period. Any period can serve as the base, depending on the intentions of the indexer. The index is usually given the value of 1.00 in the base period, and all the other periods' values follow from that. Take as an example an item with current-dollar price of $4.00 (price index 1.00) in 1992: if the price goes to $5.00 in 1993, the price index rises to 1.25; $6.00 in 1994, the index is 1.50; $5.00 in 1995, the index is 1.25.

A broad price index can be created if we average the prices of a number of different commodities together for each period. If we average together the prices of all the items in GDP, the result is called 'the price level'; the rate of change of the price level, on an annualized basis, is often referred to as the 'rate of inflation.' There is actually an even better-known measure of inflation – namely, the rate of change in the consumer price index or CPI, but that is a narrower index because it averages together only the prices of certain goods and services bought by households.

How much of the change in the GDP from one quarter to another results from a change in the physical volume of production, as opposed to rising or falling prices? Statistics Canada ('StatsCan') makes that known by publishing the volume of GDP as well as the price level every quarter, but the calculations are not as simple as one might think. For example, suppose that GDP in 1992 consisted of ten tons of steel, priced at $150 a ton, and five tons of copper, priced at $180 a ton. Its total value (the 'nominal' GDP) would be $2,400.

Now let's move to 1993, and suppose that the economy produced fifteen tons of steel at a price of $180 a ton and six tons of copper at $210 a ton. The steel was worth $2,700, and the copper, $1,260. The total value in current dollars was $2,700 plus $1,360, or $3,960. This is the current-dollar, or nominal, GDP for 1993.

StatsCan currently uses 1992 as its base year for the price level. It constructs a series called the 'real GDP' or 'constant-dollar GDP,' by taking the volumes produced each period and valuing them at 1992 prices. For 1993, for instance, the constant-dollar GDP in our little example would be computed as 15 x $150 plus 6 x $180, which is $3,330. StatsCan then computes the price-level series by dividing the nominal value by the real value in each period. In 1992 this would be 1.00, and in 1993 it would be 3,960/3,330 or 1.1892. When the price level is computed in this way, it is called the 'imputed price deflator.' The rate of inflation between 1992 and 1993 is the percentage rate of change between the price levels in the two years: in this example it would be 18.92 per cent. Table 1 illustrates the 1997 implicit price deflators, or price levels, for GDE and its major components.

Note that the implicit price deflator is calculated by weighting the prices of the individual items from each period by the volumes purchased in that period. Though the price index for 1992 reflects the volume weights for 1992, the price index for 1997 would reflect the volume weights – that is, the relative role of the items in spending patterns – five years later. Measuring inflation in this way means that the yardstick slowly changes as time goes on. Statistics Canada does publish other inflation indexes for GDP as well, using different methods for assigning the weights.

A familiar index for which the volume weights stay the same from period to period is the CPI; this is based on averaging the prices of the same selected basket of goods and services every month. Obviously, while this yardstick does not change from period to period, it does slowly get out of date, so the basket is re-selected every four years or so after a survey of household buying patterns.

In 1997, StatsCan changed its base year for calculating real GDP from 1986 to 1992. Such changes usually take place every five years or so.

Why Do Economists Emphasize 'Real' Quantities?

Economists are fond of measuring GDP in real terms or 'constant dollars,' but in the everyday world we almost always refer to the values of goods and services, and of financial assets, in nominal or money terms. Why take so much trouble to estimate volumes? The answer is that we cannot explain the behaviour of individuals, enterprises, households, and governments in terms of nominal values. Transactors actually behave as if they respond to 'real values,' even if they can observe only money prices. Basically, people are interested in goods and services because they satisfy their wants. If the prices of everything that we own, and everything else as well, rose by 20 per cent, we would not be 20 per cent better off, since we could not exchange our goods for more than before, and they would provide no more benefits to us than before.[8]

So, though the prices that we see in the stores are measured in terms of money, we act as if we were constantly, unconsciously correcting for the changing length of the money yardstick. Each of us forms an estimate of

---

8 Actually, we would be worse off, because any cash or other money-denominated assets that we have would now buy fewer goods and services than before.

inflation, primarily from recent experience, and uses it (largely unconsciously) to adjust the relative values that are reported in money terms. So, if we see that our money income has risen by 5 per cent over the last year, we mentally apply our perception of the inflation rate over the year in estimating how much better off we are, if at all. And if we are told that we can expect to receive a 4 per cent raise this year, we translate this (probably unconsciously, and not, of course, with certainty) into a sense of what it will mean for our real purchasing power.

I describe in chapter 7 how inflation expectations are formed, because they are crucial in explaining economic behaviour.

Some Relevant Economic Indicators

Most indicators are used for two purposes: first, to measure what is happening in a particular sector of the economy, and second, to suggest what is happening to the economy as a whole. Almost every indicator listed in this book has some bearing on the circular flow, but the central tables of the Canadian SNA are the **National Income and Expenditure Accounts (NIEA).**[9]

The NIEA can be reached at StatsCan's website, www.statcan.ca. The tables listed below all present the data as seasonally adjusted at annual rates (SAAR) – that is, adjusted each quarter to remove normal seasonal fluctuations. (The non-seasonally adjusted data are also provided in tables 31 to 56.)

Table 1, Gross Domestic Product, Income-based
Table 2, Gross Domestic Product, Expenditure-based
Table 3, Gross Domestic Product at 1992 Prices, Expenditure-based
Table 5, Sector Accounts – Persons and Unincorporated Businesses
Table 6, Sector Accounts – Corporations and Government Business Enterprises
Table 9, Sector Accounts – Government
Table 14, Sector Accounts – Non-Residents
Table 15, Saving, Investment and Net Lending
Table 16, Personal Expenditure on Consumer Goods and Services
Table 17, Personal Expenditure on Consumer Goods and Services at 1992 Prices
Table 19, Investment in Residential Structures, at 1992 Prices
Table 21, Investment in Non-Residential Structures and Equipment, at 1992 Prices
Table 23, Exports and Imports of Goods and Services, at 1992 Prices

---

9   The U.S. counterpart is called the **National Income and Product Accounts** (NIPA).

2

The Household Sector

In the SNA, householders play two roles. On the one hand, they are employees and consumers; on the other hand, as proprietors of small businesses, they employ people and invest in capital. StatsCan calls these the 'personal' aspect and the 'unincorporated business' aspects of the sector.

Households are a major stabilizing force in the economy. To understand how they behave, we must fit them into the circular flow described in the last chapter. Remember, from that discussion, that the producers of GDP – those who supply labour and capital – earn net domestic income (NDI), in essentially four categories: labour income, proprietors' income, investment income, and corporate and government business-enterprise profits (Table 1 and Chart 1 above). Households get most of this income, except for the profits, and if corporations declare dividends out of their profits, those flow into household income too.

Households' Sources and Uses of Funds

We should now take a look at Chart 2. The chart shows the household sector's income and outlays in 1997. Starting on the left, we see that part of personal income comes from NDI – namely, labour income, proprietors' income, and investment income. Labour income contains not just wages and salaries but also supplementary items, such as employers' contributions to pension plans and to medical plans. Proprietors' incomes arise from unincorporated businesses, including professional practices.[1] Investment income from NDI is es-

---

1 Rental income of landlords bulks larger in this item than might be expected, because Statistics Canada includes an imputed amount for rents on owner-occupied dwellings. The SNA treats homeowners as if they rent to themselves; the corresponding outlay shows up in GDE as part of consumers' expenditure on services.

Chart 2. Sources and uses of household funds

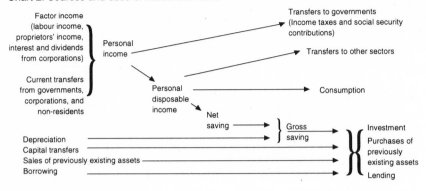

sentially interest and dividends paid by corporations to their bondholders and shareholders, but it does not include interest paid to households on their holdings of government bonds, which falls into the category of transfers (and is shown below), because such interest is not factor income. It is not included in NDI because the SNA does not in general consider governments to be producers of output.

Table 3, which pulls together the income figures, shows that over $100 billion, or 15 percent of all household income, actually came in 1997 not from NDI, but from government transfer payments. (A transfer is a payment for which no consideration is due in return, such as child benefit, employment

TABLE 3
Household income, 1997

Elements	Income ($million)
Wages, salaries, and supplementary labour income	445,924
+ Proprietors' income (income from unincorporated businesses)	54,992
+ Interest, dividends, and other investment income	85,391
+ Transfers from governments	107,016
+ Transfers from corporations and non-residents	2,713
= Personal income	696,036
− Income taxes	121,326
− Contributions to social insurance and civil service pension funds	46,933
− Transfers to corporations and non-residents	8,687
= Personal disposable income	523,711

Source: Statistics Canada, *National Income and Expenditure Accounts*, #13-001-XPB (fourth quarter 1997), Table 5.

insurance benefits, and welfare.) 'Transfers from corporations to households' represents charitable corporate contributions,[2] while 'current transfers to households by non-residents' represents funds brought with migrants as they arrive in the country.

We have now seen where 'personal income' comes from; but how do people spend it? As Table 3 shows, a major part of income is siphoned off in 'direct taxes' (mostly income taxes) and by contributions to social insurance (i.e., Canada and Quebec Pension Plans) and civil-service pension funds. What remains is called 'personal disposable income,' because households have discretion over it.

Though Table 4 looks quite complicated, households really have only three ways to use their disposable income: they can consume it, transfer it to other sectors, or save it (these are items 2, 3, and 4, respectively, in the table).[3] 'Net saving' is the residual and is often misunderstood. It should not be thought of as an active decision to do anything; it is simply what is left over from disposable income when transfers and consumption have been accounted for. This is probably not what most people think of as saving. Generally, in everyday conversation, 'saving' has the connotation of acquiring financial assets. But while saving does help to make that possible, it is not what the word means in macro-economics.

If we examine Chart 2 again, we see that apart from the three things that households can do with their disposable income, they have other transactional choices as well. As proprietors of businesses they can invest in fixed capital and inventories for the purpose of engaging in production; they can also buy pre-existing physical assets from other sectors, and they can acquire financial assets. These three activities are often referred to as 'households' uses of funds.' To finance them, they have four sources of funds in addition to their net saving: depreciation allowances that they have set aside in their businesses, net capital transfers from other sectors (most of this is wealth transferred into the country by immigrants), sales of pre-existing physical assets to other sectors, and borrowing (issuing liabilities). A sector's sources are always equal to its uses; we have now exhausted all the possibilities.

Any sector can lend to or borrow from any other sector, and any sector can sell or buy existing assets from any other sector. But the total of all the sectors' lending to each other is equal to the total of their borrowing from each other,

---

2 Charitable institutions and other non-profit organizations serving households are grouped with the household sector in the Canadian SNA.

3 Transfers from one household to another take place very frequently but do not show up in the SNA because they net out within the sector.

TABLE 4
Household outlays, 1997

Categories		$million
1 Personal disposable income		523,711
2 Consumption (personal expenditure on goods and services):		505,373
Durable goods	66,108	
Semi durable goods	45,579	
Non-durable goods	122,422	
Services	271,264	
3 Current transfers to corporations and non-residents		8,687
4 Net Saving (1–2–3)		9,651
5 Capital consumption allowances (depreciation)		27,142
6 Gross saving (4+5)		36,793
7 Net capital transfers from government and non-residents		8,215
8 Non-financial capital acquisition:		53,129
Investment in fixed capital	49,855	
Investment in inventories	−953	
Purchases of existing assets	4,227	
9 Net lending (6+7–8)		−8,121
10 Net acquisitions of financial assets:		28,215
Currency and deposits	239	
Canadian debt securities	−14,832	
Corporate shares and mutual funds	57,571	
Life insurance and pension funds	29,603	
Other financial assets	−44,366	
11 Net acquisitions of liabilities:		32,203
Consumer credit	9,747	
Bank and other loans	5,909	
Mortgages	18,767	
Trade payables	−1,897	
12 Net financial investment (10–11)		−3,988
13 Sector discrepancy (9–12)		−4,133

Source: As Table 3.

and their sales and purchases of existing assets are also equal. Since that is true, then by subtraction, the total of all the sectors' saving also equals the total of all their investment.[4]

Putting it another way, the economy as a whole cannot invest any more or less than it saves, even though individual sectors may do so. A sector that

---

4   More precisely, in terms of the Canadian SNA, all sectors' net saving and their capital consumption allowances, which together form their gross saving, are in principle equal to their investment in fixed capital and inventories. They differ only because of measurement error: the so-called statistical discrepancy. See Table 15 of the **NIEA**.

invests more than it saves (enterprises are almost always in this category) typically has to borrow from other sectors more than it lends to them. (Sales of existing assets, the other possibility, do not normally account for much.)

So we see that saving is extremely important, because there could be no investment without it.

Intermediation by Financial Markets

Chart 1 illustrates the circular flow of spending on goods and services and the incomes earned from it, but it is obviously incomplete in one major way: it does not show the sectors' lending and borrowing to and from each other, which take place primarily through the intermediation of the financial markets. Rarely these days do households lend directly; instead they may place their funds with a bank, a trust company, a credit union, or a fund management company. And though small enterprises may be financed partly by family money, most borrowing takes place through financial intermediaries as well. Financial institutions provide an invaluable service to the economy by creating and swapping financial assets and liabilities for each other and, in the process, turning one kind of risk into another.

This system makes assets palatable to groups that would otherwise be unwilling to acquire them and allows borrowers, whether households, enterprises, or governments, to undertake far more rewarding activities than they could manage otherwise. For example, since a pension fund can research the potential reward from buying corporate shares efficiently and can spread its risks through diversification, it can offer pensioners much higher rewards than they could have obtained individually. At the same time, it can provide corporate issuers of bonds and shares with financing on competitive terms, far greater than they could have accumulated from their own cash flow.

Consumption and Its Role in the Circular Flow

Now to explain how consumption is determined. I want you to start by imagining a simple world, in which households are the only sector, so that governments, enterprises, and non-residents do not exist. In this world, households make and receive no transfers and they pay no taxes, and the only expenditure on goods and services is consumption. I also neglect depreciation, so that all of GDP becomes factor income for the households that receive it. I'll refer to this factor income by the symbol 'Y.'

Everything I mention will be in 'real terms.' Admittedly, this is not intuitively straightforward. We don't see 'real' values referred to in the newspaper. The prices that we observe, the wage rates that are set, and the interest rates that are reported are almost always stated in nominal, current-dollar terms. None the less, households and other transactors do make decisions on the basis of their perceptions of real values, even if they cannot actually observe them. They desire goods and services because of their physical characteristics, not because of their money prices. If all prices doubled overnight, and everyone's money-denominated wealth doubled as well, and everyone immediately grasped what had taken place, no one would be worse or better off. They could still buy just as much value, no more or less, as before.

Of course, we are all accustomed to referring to values in money terms. We do so because money is our usual medium of transaction (that is, we exchange one good for money, then money for another good) and because money provides a convenient 'yardstick.' However, inflation shrinks the money yardstick over time at varying rates and by varying amounts relative to particular goods. This is a major inconvenience when inflation is high, because it prevents us from clearly perceiving the 'real' values in which we are interested.

To say then that people are 'really' interested in 'real' values is not to claim that they perceive them accurately. In fact, the prices of various goods and services change so erratically, and at such different rates, that people may be quite uncertain about just what their 'real' values are. None the less, though individuals may be unable to characterize their perceptions of real values confidently or precisely, they do act on them. I deal with inflation expectations again below, but for now it may make things easier to think of our imagined world as one in which individuals have no difficulty in perceiving real values.

Starting off with total (real) income of Y, we know that households either spend it on (real) consumption (C) or save it (S), since they can make no transfers (other sectors do not exist). But saving is just a residual; it is not an outlay. Therefore it does not form part of GDE, is not spent on GDP, and cannot in itself create income for anyone.

Remember that in our simple world, consumption, C, is the only component of GDE. Since GDE is made solely of C, we can go on and say that GDP will be equal to C also (since GDE and GDP are always identical quantities). Further, in this simple world where there are no transfers, GDP is the only source of household income, so we can see that households basically create their own income for themselves. That is, their consumption, C, becomes GDE, becomes GDP, becomes their income, Y.

Now let's suppose that our households receive income of Y1 in 1998. If they decide to consume less than in 1999, they will get an unpleasant shock, since the only income they will get is just what they consume – that is, their income will turn out to be lower in 1999 than it was the year before. If,

Chart 3. Households' consumption and expected income

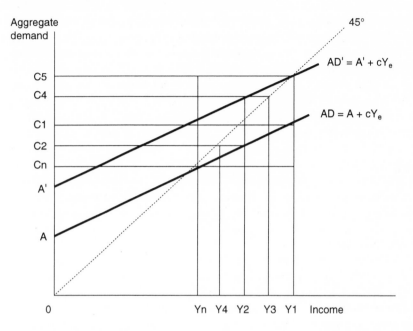

however, they then consume more in 2000, their incomes will rise correspond-ingly in that year as well.

Suppose that in each successive period they start out by expecting their income to be what it actually was in the previous period. In 1999, then, they will expect to receive the amount of income they actually received in 1998, say Y1; but if they plan to consume only part of this (say Y2) and save the rest, they will create themselves only Y2 of income. In 2000, having adjusted their income expectations downward, they will expect to earn Y2; but once again, their expectations will be thwarted if they consume more or less than this.

It is a 'great simplification' of macro-economics that aggregate consumption does depend on expected income. Unfortunately, we cannot actually look into individuals' minds to find out what they expect their income to be, and StatsCan does not publish any estimates of this amount. Macro-economists, not surprisingly, have spent a tremendous amount of time and effort trying to find appropriate ways of estimating the expected income that motivates consumption. Generally, it is useful to think of wealth, in a broad sense, as a major driver of expected income, but this takes us into complex issues that we can't discuss here. For now, I suggest that you can get a very long way on the proposition that aggregate income can be proxied relatively simply by the last period's actual personal income. It is very far from a perfect measure, but for our purposes it can be a good approximation.

So we start off with two simplifying propositions for our little world. First, 'expected income' for each period, which we can call 'Y_e,' we assume to be equal to last period's actual income. (We can call actual income 'Y_a' so the symbol for last period's actual income would be Y_{a-1}.)' Second, though aggregate consumption, C, depends mostly on expected income, it depends also on many other factors as well. However, trying to take account of them would complicate the story greatly, and since they are of less importance generally, we will not try to explain them.

Typically, when expected income increases, consumption rises too, by a large fraction of that expected income. Economists call this fraction, which we will label 'c,' 'the marginal propensity to consume' (MPC). Since we are not trying to explain the rest of consumption, we can just give the remainder a name, 'A.' Thus $C = A + cY_e$.

Refer now to Chart 3. In this chart, the horizontal axis represents income, Y, and the vertical axis represents spending on goods and services, or GDE. (The axis is labelled 'aggregate demand,' which is just another name for GDE. The scales are drawn to be identical, so any point on a 45° line from the origin represents a situation where expected income and expenditure are identical.)

We now illustrate the behaviour of household consumption in the following way. Y_e (i.e., expected income, on the horizontal axis) gives rise to consumption of C, composed of $A + cY_e$, measured on the vertical axis. The amount of C at various levels of Y_e appears as an upward-sloping line, which we label as $AD = A + cY_e$. (The slope, c, is upward, because c is positive, but it is flatter than the 45° line, because c is less than 1.) (We can refer to aggregate demand as AD, which is just another symbol for GDE. In the simple world that we are discussing at the moment, however, consumption is the only form of expenditure.)

Suppose that expected income starts off at a level of Y1. If this were so, how much would households consume? Reading up to the consumption line (identified as $AD = A + cY_e$), we see that they will consume an amount equal to C1 on the vertical axis, which is below the intersection with the 45° line. Since there is no other expenditure going on, C1 constitutes all of GDE for this period. How much income does this expenditure create? Since GDE equals GDP and GDP equals Y_a, all of the expenditure becomes income; and since the two axes' scales are the same, we can translate expenditure of C1 on the vertical axis into the income Y2 on the horizontal axis. So, though households were expecting to receive income of Y1, they actually receive income of only Y2 (because they are both the consumers and the producers in this little economy; their income depends directly on what they spend).

How much will be consumed in the next period? Since consumption is based on expected income, and expected income is equal to last period's actual income, the 'Y_e' in '$A + cY_e$' this time will be Y2 (that is, the first period's actual income), which is smaller than Y1. So total consumption will shrink to C2, read off the line labelled $AD = A + cY_e$, which is less than the C1 of consumption that took place in the first period, and it creates actual income of only Y4. And so on.

You should be able to see, however, that the chain does not end at an income of zero. Once income has fallen to Yn, the consumption line at that level of income will have reached Cn, which will re-create the same level of income, Yn, over again. (In a similar fashion, if we had started out in the first period with an expected income level below Yn, consumption would have been above the 45° line, households would have consumed more than their expected income, and their actual income would have gravitated towards Yn, where it would stabilize.) This is the way in which households' behaviour tends to stabilize the economy.

In our illustrated example, how much have households saved? It turns out that they have saved nothing. In the first period, for instance, they expected to receive income of Y1, and based on that they consumed C1, intending to save the difference, Y1–C1. But they did not actually get to save it, because the income that they actually received was only Y2. Until their income fell to Yn, in fact, their income expectations were continually disappointed, and they were never able to save at all. This is another way in which saving is 'residual' – it is the part that either falls short of or exceeds intentions when actual income turns out to be lower or higher than expected.

Now, looking once more at the diagram, suppose that the 'A' part of consumption (the part that we are not trying to explain) increases arbitrarily from A to some larger amount A' and stays there each period. This would be appear on the diagram as a shift from the lower to the higher of the heavy bold lines. Given this situation, what would happen if we started out with an expected income of Yn? The answer is that households would consume C1, which is more than Yn (how would they be able to do this? The simplest assumption is that they give each other credit). This expenditure would create income of Y2. Starting out in the next period, expecting this larger amount of income, their consumption would rise, and the process would continue until income rose to

Y1, with consumption of C3. At this point, the system has arrived at a new equilibrium. In the absence of further shifts in A (or in c, the slope of the heavy line, the MPC), the level of income would remain at this level from now on.

The Multiplier

The exercise has shown that an increase in autonomous spending (in this case, from A to A') leads to an increase in the equilibrium level of income, from Yn to Y1. The increase in the latter is greater than the increase in the former! We seem to have created something out of nothing – we start with a consumption increase amounting to the difference between A' and A but end up with an income increase of Y1 minus Yn, which is a considerably bigger amount. Since, in every period,

(1) $Y_a = A + cY_e$ (that is, actual income is equal to consumption),

so, by subtraction,

(2) $Y_a - cY_e = A$.

When we have reached equilibrium, then Y_a will be equal to Y_e. Therefore, at equilibrium,

(3) $Y - cY = A$, and

(4) $Y(1 - C) = A$, or

(5) $Y = 1/(1 - c)A$

Therefore if A changes by an arbitrary amount X, it will bring about a change in the equilibrium level of Y equal to $1/(1 - c)$ times X. Since we multiply the change in A by $1/(1 - c)$ to get the change in equilibrium income, macroeconomists call the expression $1/(1 - c)$ the 'multiplier.'

Fluctuations in A (or, for that matter, in other components of GDE, such as investment, government spending, and exports, introduced below, as we go to a fuller, more realistic model), do not change the equilibrium level of GDP by just their own amount; they have a multiplied effect on it. This means that when households receive an increase in income, they spend more on consumption, which adds further to income, which increases consumption, which adds to income, ... until the process exhausts itself, with income stabilized at a new level. In reality, however, the process never does exhaust itself, because there is always some new factor that enters the situation; the economy is always moving towards equilibrium but never actually reaches it.

Making Sense of the Real World

In the real world, of course, aggregate consumption is not just a simple function of aggregate income. For one thing, governments levy taxes on income, and they also make transfers to households such as Old Age Security. If we add transfers to households' factor income, but subtract direct taxes, we get a more useful measure of what households can actually control; StatsCan does measure this; it is called 'personal disposable income.' But households do not consume a fixed percentage of their disposable income either. Some of the variability in this relationship depends on the confidence with which they view their earning prospects. They appear to be willing to consume a much higher proportion of income that they consider stable or reliable than they will from windfalls. Disposable income that households consider sustainable and predictable calls forth a strong, high consumption response (a high 'c'). Conversely, income that they consider transient influences consumption much less.

The Role of Wealth

Chart 4 shows that consumption has actually grown faster than disposable income in the 1980s and 1990s. Putting it another way, net saving has fallen sharply. Does this mean that households are on a spending binge? Or that they think their current disposable income is not a realistic reflection of their true spending power? The latter interpretation has some merit. The chart illustrates that household net worth has grown faster than income over the same period, and there is no question that households as a whole have become far wealthier. Though household debt has risen very quickly, household assets, both financial and physical, have expanded far more. In fact, wealth may correlate better with the 'expected sustainable income' that drives consumption than StatsCan's actual measure of personal disposable income. The dispersion of income and wealth between wealthy and poor has also widened; the subject is well worth pursuing, but it is beyond our scope.

The Components of Consumer Spending

StatsCan identifies four major components of consumer expenditure on goods and services. As Chart 5 shows, *services* represent the largest category, a

Chart 4. Households' net worth, disposable income, and consumption, 1981–97

Indexed, 1981 =100

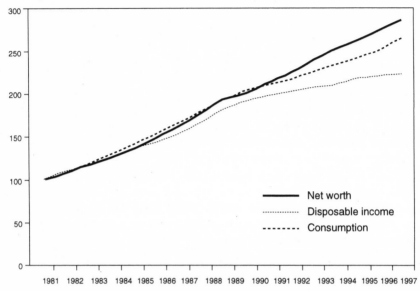

Sources: Statistics Canada, CANSIM database, series D160003, D14817, D14914.

diverse group that includes rent, restaurants and accommodation, financial and legal services, recreation, personal and medical care, and a number of other items. *Non-durable goods* (such as food and beverages, fuels and electricity) have accounted for a slowly falling share of spending over the years, whereas the share of *semi-durables* (such as clothing and footwear) has remained relatively stable. *Durable goods* (items generally expected to be used over a period of three years or more, such as cars, furniture, and appliances) deserve a little further exploration. Capital items purchased by households for business use should of course be considered investment, not consumption, but the SNA does not classify them as such because of the difficulty of distinguishing them. Durables' long period of use and the fact that they are often 'big-ticket' items means that the cost of financing them substantially affects the purchase decision. This fact makes them different from other types of consumption, which are for the most part relatively insensitive to real interest rates.

Chart 5. Consumption trends relative to GDP, 1980–97

% of GDP

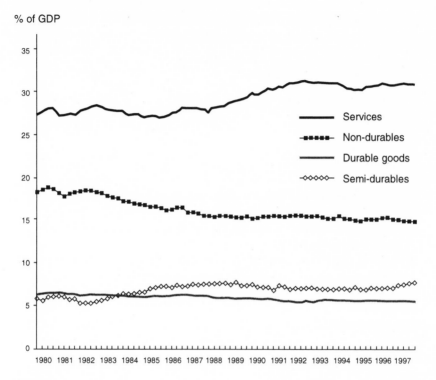

Imports

A good part of consumption involves imported goods and services. This represents a leakage out of the economy's circular flow, and it reduces the value of the multiplier. When we discuss transactions with non-residents in chapter 6, we come to terms with the role of exchange rates in determining the distribution of consumption between imports and domestically produced goods and services.

Housing Investment

Households actually contribute more than consumption to the expenditure side of the circular flow. They also invest, in their role as landlords, in housing. I briefly discuss investment in residential construction in the next chapter.

Useful Economic Indicators

All indicators appear monthly unless indicated otherwise: (Q) = quarterly; (W) = weekly.

Canada

Average Hourly Earnings
Car Sales
Consumer Price Index
Employment and Unemployment
Financial Flow Accounts (Q)
Help-Wanted Index
Household Credit (W) (in **Bank of Canada Weekly Financial Statistics**)
Housing Starts
National Balance Sheet Accounts (NBSA) (Q) (table for personal and
    unincorporated business sector)
National Income and Expenditure Accounts (NIEA) (Q) (table for Personal
    and Unincorporated Business Sector, Personal Outlays on Consumption,
    and Residential Construction)
Retail Trade
Wage Settlements

United States

Car Sales
Consumer Credit
Consumer Price Index
Employment and Unemployment
Employment Cost Index (Q)
Help-Wanted Index
Housing Starts
Initial State Unemployment Insurance Claims (W)
Personal Income
Retail Sales

3

The Enterprise Sector

Now we move from households to enterprises. Enterprises are the instruments of a capitalist society for deciding what to produce and how to produce it. As consumers' preferences change, entrepreneurs offer new goods and services, change the characteristics of old ones, and try out new prices for their products. They are also constantly experimenting with new ways to produce, responding to changing relative input prices and to new technological possibilities. This ceaseless experimentation is costly and risky, but it carries high potential reward. Entrepreneurs' central contribution to the market economy is their unending effort to find new and more satisfactory solutions to the 'what and how' questions, enticed by the lure of substantial profits. Of course, in an open, competitive economy, profits are hard to protect for long, since other entrepreneurs keep emerging to offer cheaper and better products and services.

Macro-economics does not, however, dwell on this innovative characteristic of the enterprise. It concentrates on the aggregate production function and the role of business investment as a component of aggregate demand. A production function describes the relation between inputs and output. In other words, it answers the question, 'How does output change when inputs vary?' Let us consider a single firm that produces a single good, using only two factors of production, which we can call 'labour' (L) and 'capital goods' (K). We assume that the enterprise knows the cost of labour (which we can call the real wage), the real interest rate,[1] the price of capital goods, and the demand for its product. Given this information, it must decide how much output to produce and

---

1 Expected real interest rates represent the difference between nominal interest rates and the rate of inflation expected over the relevant period. If you can earn 5 per cent nominally over a year but you expect inflation to be 3 per cent, your expected real rate of return is only about 2 per cent (1.05/1.03 = 1.0194).

the amounts of each factor to employ in making it. From micro-economics we know that the firm chooses a level of production that equates its marginal cost to its marginal revenue – i.e., the level where the last unit produced generates only as much additional revenue as it adds to cost. (As in the previous chapter, we carry on our discussion in 'real terms.' Though the uncertainty of inflation expectations influences the choices that firms make, we can neglect this factor here.)

For any particular level of output, the firm would want to use the least-cost combination of factor inputs. Looking at Chart 6, we see that the firm could produce output at level 1 in many different ways – for instance, by using L3 units of labour and K1 units of capital, L2 of labour and K2 of capital, or L1 units of labour and K3 of capital. If it decides to produce this level of output, its choice of factors would turn on their relative marginal costs: the higher the real wage, the less labour it would use (for a given real cost of capital); the higher the real cost of capital, the less capital it would use (for a given real wage). (The 'real wage' here is total expected labour compensation per period worked.)

Chart 6. The relationship between inputs and outputs

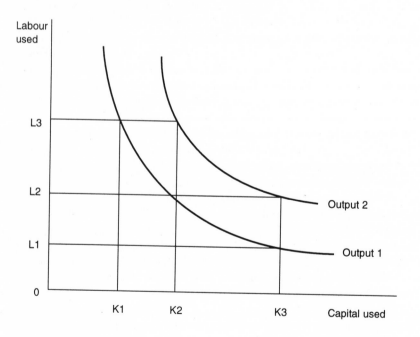

Chart 7. Determining the desired capital stock

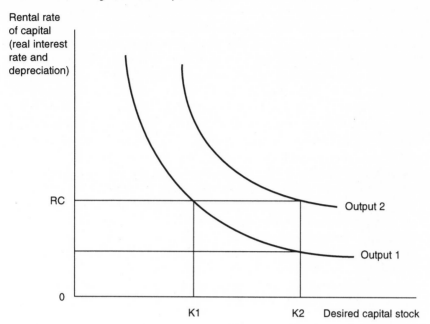

In the case of capital, the notion of 'cost' is a little complicated. As with labour, it is the services of capital, not the capital good itself, that are wanted. But the cost (called the 'real rental rate') of the services of capital depends not only on the price of the machine or structure in question but also on the real interest rate and the depreciation rate (Chart 7).

Assume that P_k is the price of a new machine. If r is the real interest rate, then r times P_k is the amount that must be paid to a lender to borrow the funds needed to rent the machine for a year. And if d is the rate of depreciation, then d times P_k is the amount required to offset wear and tear over a year. The total rental cost of capital on an annualized basis is thus (r+d) times P_k.

What would happen if the real interest rate rose, assuming that everything else remained the same? This would clearly increase the real rental rate of capital, so it would lead firms to use more labour, and less capital, to produce any given level of output.

Relationship between Desired Stock and Investment Rate

Once the firm has worked out the lowest-cost combination of labour and capital for any given level of output, and has chosen both its desired level of output and the amounts of labour and capital services that it would like to employ, it has an investment decision to make – how quickly it should close the gap, or bring its stock of capital from whatever level it has previously owned up to the desired level.

Firms do not always, or even typically, close this gap fully within a single period. The lag between order and delivery may be long. The processes of installation, operator training, and run-in may also be lengthy. So firms often spread the investment spending related to a particular gap over a number of periods. But as time passes, new information and new circumstances will certainly arise; for example, the going real wage may change, different real interest rates may appear in the financial markets, and shifts may occur in the demand for the firm's own product. These changes will alter the desired level of capital services, as well as of labour. So, even before the original gap has been closed, the enterprise will set about closing a new one. The amount of investment spending that takes place during any given period can be thought of as a response to a series of past gaps.

Investment as a Component of Aggregate Demand

Up to this point we have looked at investment decisions in relation to the production functions of individual firms. Macro-economics uses analogous reasoning to explain aggregate investment. We can imagine an aggregate production function, where the output is real GDP, and the factor inputs are the economy's labour force and its stock of fixed capital – i.e., its equipment and structures.

In the SNA, the term 'gross fixed investment' refers to outlays on the production, alteration, and improvement of capital goods (machinery, equipment, and residential, commercial, and industrial buildings and structures, excluding land, which is not produced). It includes the costs of ownership transfers (for example, the value of commissions on real estate transactions and transfer taxes), because these form part of the purchase price, even though commissions are strictly payments for services, not for goods. Gross fixed investment adds to the value of the capital stock, but depreciation and scrappage reduce it.[2] The difference is net fixed investment.

---

2   In the SNA, 'investment' extends beyond outlays on fixed capital such as buildings and equipment to include the value of the physical change, from one period to the next, in inventories of raw materials, work-in-progress, and finished goods.

Investment and Real Interest Rates

In assessing the prospects for aggregate investment, forecasters pay a great deal of attention to real interest rates. They do so partly because (as mentioned above) the rates are a driving element in the process, and partly because policy-makers at a nation's central bank can influence these rates, and thus affect the level of investment spending. Economists have put a great deal of effort into identifying and estimating the relationship between real interest rates and aggregate investment spending. At the level of the firm, it is clear that a rise in the real rental rate of capital tends to reduce the desired level of capital services and therefore make for a smaller gap. It could also lead a firm to stretch out the time it plans to take to close a given gap.

But it is not easy to identify and characterize these relationships at the aggregate level, because 'capital' is a diverse group of assets, the gaps overlap, and it is not clear exactly how interest rates affect the analysis. For example, a rise in real interest rates may be taken as a signal of tightening monetary policy, which might lead firms to reduce their expectations about future levels of demand for their output, as well as to recognize that it is now more expensive to borrow. It may also lead lenders to draw the same conclusion, prompting them to tighten their credit standards and impose tougher conditions on would-be borrowers. So it may not be just the borrowers' own criteria that are relevant to the relationship between rates and investment.

In any case, we can presume that a rise in real interest rates reduces the rate of investment, as firms respond to it. This we can think of as the second 'great simplification' of macro-economics.

Let us now add this second component of aggregate demand, investment, to the one discussed above, consumption. Whereas I portrayed consumption as sensitive to expected income, investment is sensitive to real interest rates. But while the relationship between disposable income and consumption is positive, that between interest rates and investment is negative.

In the last chapter, I characterized consumption as having two components – one sensitive to expected income, and the other (less important) accounting for all the other influences that may be at work. In the same way we can think of investment as having two parts – one responsive negatively to the real rate of interest, and the other driven by whatever other unrelated influences may play upon it. In symbols we could say that I is equal to F plus b times r, where F is the part unrelated to interest rates, b a negative coefficient, and r 'the' real interest rate.[3]

---

3   Of course, there is not just a single real interest rate; a structure of rates applies to a variety of borrowers, representing the costs of borrowing for various periods of time. I use 'r' just as short hand for the entire structure of rates confronting enterprises.

Change in Investment and Aggregate Demand

In the previous chapter, we saw that a once-for-all shift in the autonomous component of consumption, A (for example, from A to A'), leads to a larger shift in aggregate demand and the equilibrium level of income (NDI and GDP), through the so-called multiplier process. The very same process multiplies the impact of a change in investment spending as well. If the rate of investment shifts, as a result of a change in real interest rates or for any other reason, the equilibrium level of aggregate demand and income shifts by a multiplied amount, just as when it reacts to shifts in A.

Taking over the 45° diagram from the previous chapter, we can add investment to it. Let us suppose that real interest rates are at the level r (Chart 8). Aggregate demand, AD, measured on the vertical axis, will now be represented by the heavy line labelled $A + F + cY_e + br$ ($A + cY_e$ is consumption; $F + br$ is investment). Note that the slope of the line is still given by c; that is, the investment component of spending does not vary with the level of expected income, so it just adds a fixed amount to aggregate demand each period, whatever expected income may be.

As above, we assume that there is no government (so no transfers or taxes) and no non-resident sector (so no imports and exports), but enterprises now exist and invest. We also continue to assume that households revise their expected level of income each period to reflect the actual income received in the previous period. If we happen to start out with an expected income of Y0, aggregate demand will be AD0. This becomes the income of that period, which turns out to be Y0 again – this is an equilibrium situation.[4]

Suppose, however, that the real interest rate falls from r to r' at the beginning of period 2 and remains there. This will lead enterprises to increase their investment spending in response, from F + br to F + br'. We represent this change by shifting the AD curve upward by the same amount all along its length, labelling the new curve AD'. Aggregate demand in period 2 shifts upward from AD0 to AD1 – that is, by the amount of additional investment. By inspection of the diagram we can see that this will generate income of Y1 (the horizontal distance 0Y1 is equal to the vertical distance 0AD1.)

---

4   Actually, as gross investment proceeds over a number of periods, it will tend to close the gap between enterprises' desired level of capital stock and the amount with which they started. As the gap closes, the rate of investment itself could fall. And the rate at which the gap is closed depends not only on the cumulative amount of gross investment but also on the rate at which the existing stock is depreciated or scrapped. Our analysis here takes the size of the aggregate gap as given, which is a reasonable assumption only because we are limiting ourselves to considering the short-run response of investment to changes in real interest rates.

Chart 8. Role of investment in aggregate demand

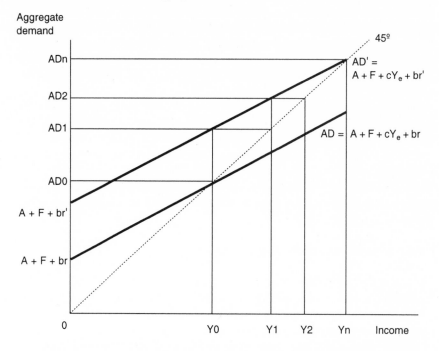

At the start of the third period, the level of expected income, which is equal to the income received in the previous period, has thus grown to Y1. In response, consumption increases from its previous level by c times (Y1–Y0). (We are still on the curve labelled AD', but now we have moved upward along it to a higher level, which we can label AD2.) In turn, this generates income of Y2, ... and the process will continue in an upward spiral until we reach an income of Yn. At this point, since the AD' curve crosses the 45° line here, spending, at ADn, will be just equal to the expected income, Yn, that gives rise to it and thus will give rise to itself again. In other words, we have reached a new equilibrium level of income Yn, considerably higher than the original Y0.

Note that the difference between Y0 and Yn is much greater than that between Y0 and Y1. In other words, though the disturbance to the equilibrium level of income was caused by an upward shift in investment spending, it was augmented (or multiplied) by the shift in consumption that took place in response. Here again we have the multiplier process. The effect of the increase in investment is analogous to the effect of the rise in autonomous consumption examined in chapter 2. Because the growth in the equilibrium level of income is equal to $1/(1-c)$ times the increase in investment, we can express the multiplier as $1/(1-c)$.

Obviously, the size of the multiplier depends on the size of c, which is the marginal propensity to consume or MPC. If the MPC is large (for example, 0.9), the multiplier will be large too; in this case it would be equal to $1/(1-0.9)$, or 10. If the MPC is small (for example, 0.6) then the multiplier would be small as well; in this case, $1/(1-0.6)$, or 2.5.

In summary, the size of the economy can be very sensitive to investment decisions, which are themselves sensitive to real interest rates, because the response of consumption to changes in expected income tends to multiply the effect of any shift in investment. None the less, the economy does not tend to fall into ever-widening fluctuations; rather, it tends to gravitate towards a particular level of aggregate demand. (As a practical matter, however, with new information and new developments arising every period, equilibrium is never actually reached.)

Why Must Investment Be Equal to Saving?

We have now added investment to the expenditure mix, but in the last chapter I pointed out that investment must always be equal to saving, at least for the economy as a whole. But as we have seen, investment is sensitive to interest rates, while consumption (and the residual, saving) are sensitive mostly to income. Most of the time, in fact, enterprises invest more than they save, and households save more than they invest. What is it that forces S to be equal to I for the whole economy?

The answer is that if, in aggregate, investment spending exceeds the amount of saving that was intended, then saving too will turn out to be higher than was intended. Saving, which is just a residual, changes permissively: it will turn out to be higher than intended when actual income exceeds the amount that was expected and lower than intended when income falls short of expectations. In our simplified world, where we are dealing only with households and enterprises, it is they who save more or less than they had expected to; but in the real world, where governments and non-residents complete the picture, it may turn out that one or both of these sectors provides the saving that equates the economy's total to its investment.

After the fact, then, investment will always turn out to have been equal to saving, if we take the economy as a whole, but this does not mean that investment intentions are the same as saving intentions. Rather, it is the amount of saving that adjusts itself upward or downward, to equate to the amount of investment that has been carried out.

In fact, this is how the economy grows or contracts. If investment exceeds saving intentions, then GDE and income will be larger than they were expected to be, and saving will rise to make up the difference. If investment falls short of saving intentions, then GDE will turn out to be lower than its previous level, and saving too will be less than planned.

Are there, then, no constraints on investment? Not really. Assuming that financial intermediaries are functioning well, those who wish to borrow to finance investment will confront a structure of real interest rates, and we know that this will influence their decisions. So we must turn in due course to the factors that drive interest rates, to fill out the story behind investment.

Recent Investment in the Canadian Economy

Investment spending strongly affects fluctuations in aggregate demand. The decision to replace or refurbish capital equipment and structures depends on many potentially volatile factors, of which real interest rates are only one. The stronger anticipated aggregate demand is, the more firms wish to meet it with additional capacity; the higher the cost of labour, the more rapidly firms shift to capital-intensive methods of production or distribution; structures and complex machinery generally take much longer to acquire than computers or trucks; and there is a complex feedback affect among changing technologies, evolving consumer desires, and firms' anxieties not to be left behind.

All these factors make the 'F' in the investment equation volatile and very hard to predict, and since investment is itself volatile, it tends to transmit that volatility to AD through the multiplier process. If the Bank of Canada wishes to encourage stronger or weaker economic growth for the sake of keeping inflation close to target, however, one way it can do so is to lower or raise real interest rates, counting on their influence to strengthen or weaken investment outlays in the following quarters.

Investment spending has a longer-term influence on the economy as well, since it not only adds to the stock of physical capital but also renews and modernizes it, replacing and augmenting stock that has become obsolescent or has deteriorated with time and use. The larger and more modern the capital stock, the higher the economy's potential output, other things being equal; we assess the implications of this relationship in chapter 7.

Residential Construction

Housing expenditures are a major component of aggregate demand (see Chart 9 and Table 5). Over time, purchases of new housing account for about half of

Chart 9. Investment outlays by type, 1980–97

Millions of 1992 dollars
(SAAR)

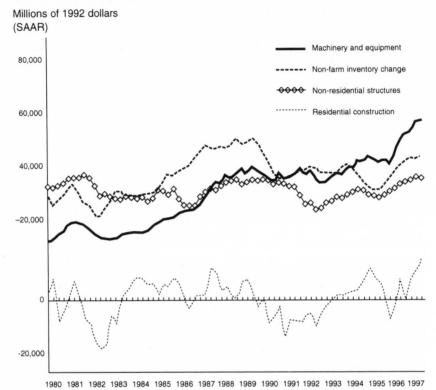

Sources: Statistics Canada, *National Income and Expenditure Accounts* #13-001-XPB
(fourth quarter 1997), Table 3.

residential construction outlays. Transfer costs account for another sixth, and
alterations and improvements to the existing housing stock make up the remaining third. Investment in new housing units is much more volatile than the
other two components. Since it is easily postponed and represents a momentous decision for a household, it is very sensitive to interest rates and consumers'
confidence, as well as to trends in family formation.

Non-residential Construction

Non-residential structures typically have a long expected working life and are
normally financed with relatively long-term debt. Decisions to construct are
sensitive to long-term interest rates, because the purchaser will commit himself

TABLE 5
Investment outlays in Canada, 1997

Outlay	A $million (current dollars)	B $million (1992 dollars)	A/B Implicit price deflator, 1992 = 1.00
Residential construction	46,091	43,038	1.071
New housing construction	22,264	21,967	1.014
Alterations and improvements	15,883	13,471	1.179
Ownership transfer costs	7,944	7,600	1.045
Non-residential structures	53,257	49,675	1.072
Building: governments	5,962	5,411	1.102
Building: business	13,220	12,093	1.093
Engineering: government	8,065	7,627	1.057
Engineering: business	26,010	24,544	1.060
Machinery and equipment			
Government	4,088	4,596	0.889
Business	55,130	52,586	1.048
Inventory change			
Government	5	4	
Business	6,610	6,192	

Source: Statistics Canada, National Income and Expenditure Accounts, #13-001-XPB, fourth quarter 1997, Tables 18, 19, 20, 21.

or herself to servicing the financing for many years. The lag between a decision to build and the actual outlay on the asset is typically very long, and the outlay itself is usually spread over a number of quarters. As Chart 9 illustrates, non-residential construction has not grown with the economy during the 1980s and 1990s. Its significant decline, relative to GDE as a whole, is in large measure a response to the relatively high level of real long-term interest rates that Canada has experienced for the last two decades.

Machinery and Equipment

Outlays on machinery and equipment have been one of the strongest-growing components of GDE for the last few decades, for two reasons in particular. First, these assets have shorter average useful lives than structures do, and so investment in them is more sensitive to shorter-term real interest rates, which have fallen in the 1990s relative to long-term rates (see Chart 10). Second, there has been an explosion of spending on computers, itself driven by the remarkable rate of increase in their capability per dollar spent on them. (StatsCan accounts for this increase by imputing a declining price to this asset category,

Chart 10. Real interest rates, 1980–97
Percentage

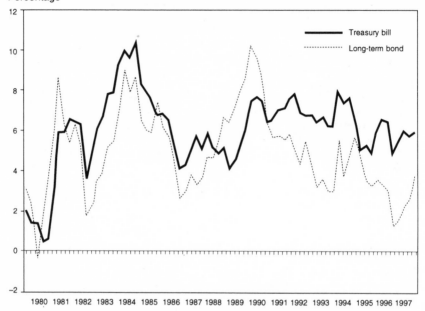

Sources: Statistics Canada, CANSIM database, Series B14007, B14013, and D15612.
Average nominal interest rate divided by rate of change in GDP deflator.

so that for a given amount spent in current dollars, the 'volume' of computers purchased rises from one year to the next.)

Inventory Investment

The value of physical change in business inventories is reported separately for the farm and the non-farm sectors. It can of course be negative, and Chart 9 shows that stocks have indeed tended to be cut during recessions (which makes the recessions worse). (Note that Statistics Canada reports the value of the physical change in inventories, not the change in the value of inventories held. Since GDE measures expenditures on current production, it must exclude changes in value that simply reflect the repricing of previously existing stocks.)

Key Economic Indicators

Corporate Profits (quarterly)
Durable Goods Orders (monthly)
Real interest rates

From a forecasting point of view, given that investment is such a heterogeneous aggregation of outlays, it is fruitless to attempt to project it with accuracy. A shift in the structure of real interest rates, however, usually calls forth a significant investment response over a number of quarters if it is not soon reversed. Strength in corporate profits is also associated with strength in investment, not so much because it means that firms can substitute internal funding for borrowing as because it tends to indicate strong product demand and thus leads entrepreneurs to take a more optimistic view of future demand.

Real interest rates I discuss more fully in chapter 7 as an instrument of monetary policy. It is important to adjust the nominal interest rates observable in the financial markets by an estimate of the likely rate of inflation over the relevant future period. A forecaster, of course, wants not his or her own expectations but rather an estimate of the market consensus. Since market expectations are unknown, it is conventional to proxy them by recent inflation, for example, for the latest year; studies suggest that the 'expectations' embedded in nominal interest rates do indeed appear to be related to recent inflation experience.

4

The Government Sector

The Rapid Growth of Government in the Economy

Charts 11 and 12, which refer to all the levels of government taken together, make clear how dramatically their role in the economy has increased in recent decades. Governments' capital spending did not contribute to this expansion (outlays on roads, schools, airports, and so on peaked in the 1960s as a factor in the economy), and capital transfers (subsidies to business to encourage investment) have not been a major growth area. But the public sector expanded sharply in the late 1960s, followed by a massive increase in transfer programs from the early 1970s onward and finally by sharp growth in interest payments on the public debt in the 1980s. However, the events of the 1990s have at least temporarily reversed the trend.

While governments' tax revenues and investment income (the shaded area in Chart 11) more or less kept pace with outlays until the mid-1970s, they failed to do so after that. Year after year deficits built a growing public debt, worsened further by rising interest payments, which were especially explosive during periods of high interest rates in the 1980s and early 1990s. Finally the situation became politically intolerable, and both federal and provincial levels of government began to take severe measures to restrain their outlays and bolster their revenues.

Chart 12 illustrates the sources of revenue on which governments have drawn to meet their rising needs. Income taxes on corporate and government business enterprises fell, not rose, through the period. Indirect taxes, including the federal goods and services tax (GST) and provincial sales taxes (PST), have remained relatively stable relative to GDP. Evidently, the major revenue elasticity came from personal income taxes and social security contributions, which between them rose from just over 7 per cent of GDP in 1961 to roughly 20 per cent in 1997.

Chart 11. Governments' revenues and outlays as % of GDP, 1961–97

% of GDP

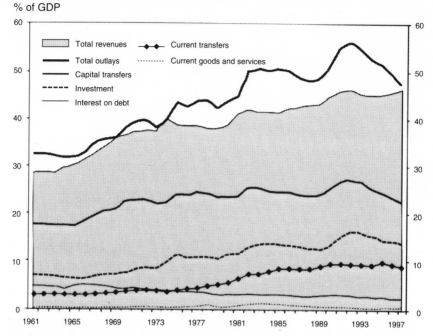

Source: Statistics Canada, *National Income and Expenditure Accounts*, #13-001-XPB
(fourth quarter, 1997), Table 9; data plotted annually.

How Governments Enter the Circular Flow

Refer back to Chart 1 in chapter 1. Governments enter the circular flow directly, through their own outlays on currently produced goods and services (we can call them 'G'), and also indirectly, through their transfers to households and businesses ('TR') and through the taxes that they levy on households, businesses, and non-residents ('T').

The size of G is determined by political choices, and no simple generalization can explain it. As a component of GDE, it includes expenditures on items for current use (including civil service salaries) and also investment in capital (for example, bridges, roads, and schools). It does not include interest paid on government debt, which does not appear in NDI either; the SNA treats such interest as a transfer to bondholders rather than factor income, since it is not a reward for a contribution to a production activity, unlike interest paid on corporate bonds.

Chart 12. Governments' revenues as % of GDP, 1961–97

% of GDP

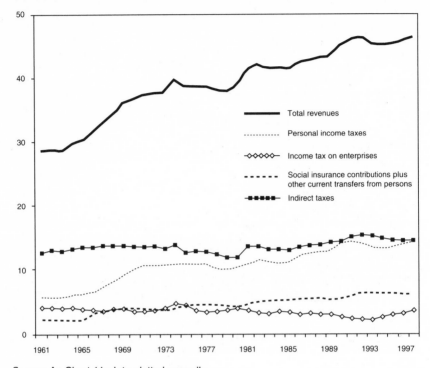

Source: As Chart 11; data plotted annually.

TR is not included in GDE either, because TR does not involve purchasing goods and services. As a result, TR does not generate factor income. Instead, like interest on government bonds, TR constitutes part of the non-factor income of the sectors that receive it.

There are two major types of taxes – direct and indirect. Direct taxes are, at least in theory, remitted directly by the party that owes the tax; personal and corporate income taxes are good examples. In the circular flow, they show up as a payment out of household and enterprise income (see Chart 1). In contrast, 'indirect' taxes, such as GST, PST, customs duties, and excise taxes, being part of the prices paid for goods and services (and remitted by those who collect them, rather than by those who pay them), are included in the value of GDE and GDP. Since the producers of GDP do not get to keep these taxes, we subtract them from GDP (whereas subsidies are an addition, like a negative indirect tax) in order to arrive at GDP at factor cost.

What happens when G, TR, and T enter the circular flow? Let us continue with the discussion of the simple world introduced above in chapter 2, continuing to omit such complexities as depreciation and dealings with non-residents. At the outset, we also exclude indirect taxes; for now, 'T' refers only to direct taxes, including social security contributions.

Now that we are including government spending on goods and services, G, in the circular flow, the expenditure side, GDE (or aggregate demand, AD) becomes the sum of C + I + G, rather than simply C + I.

But we need to analyse C a little more closely. Earlier, we had derived an expression for it in terms of expected income – namely, $C = A + cY_e$. (The subscripted 'e' distinguishes expected income from actual income, for which I will use the subscript 'a'). With government in the picture, the situation has become more complex. In addition to Y_e (which refers only to expected factor incomes), households now have incomes in the form of transfers (TR) as well and also pay income taxes and social security contributions (T). So we can rewrite the expression for consumption as follows: $C = A + c(Y + TR - T)_e$. The expression $(Y + TR - T)_e$ represents expected 'personal disposable income.' In other words, we now have to recognize that the income that drives consumption includes not only factor earnings but transfers and that we must subtract income taxes from both in order to arrive at personal disposable income. Households, in other words, base their consumption decisions on their expected income including transfers and minus income taxes and social security contributions.

One implication of this situation is that government outlays will have quite a different impact on the economy depending on how they are spent. If governments increase G, the effect on GDE will be similar to that of an increase in investment. That is, the increase in the equilibrium level of GDE will equal the increase in G times the multiplier. But an increase in transfers is a different matter. These do not enter GDE or GDP directly but simply add to incomes. By increasing household incomes, they do tend to increase consumption, but households plan to consume only a portion of any increase in their disposable income, saving the rest. So the increase in C that they cause will be equal not to the full increase in TR, but only to c times the increase. (This equation refers to the first-period response. The increase in consumption will of course create more income itself, and the multiplier will then carry on, spiralling GDP upward towards its new equilibrium through a number of periods.)

The effect of a change in T – that is, in direct taxes – resembles that of a change in transfers but has the opposite sign. Whereas transfers increase households' disposable incomes, taxes reduce them, so the fall in consumption that follows from an increase in T will equal c times the change in T – symbolically, $c(\Delta T)$. Again, further decline follows over succeeding periods, as GDP spirals downward to a new equilibrium level.

It may be useful to characterize these relationships symbolically. Before government was introduced, we had

(1) $C + I = AD = Y_a$.

So, substituting for C,

(2) $A + cY_e + I = AD = Y_a$,

where the subscript e denotes 'expected' and the subscript a denotes 'actual.'

Now that government is in the picture, however,

(3) $C + I + G = AD = Y_a$.

or, equivalently,

(4) $A + c (Y + TR - T)_e + I + G = Y_a$.

If we assume that governments levy taxes as a constant proportion, t, of factor income Y, then, letting t stand for T/Y, we could write, instead of (4),

(5) $A + c (Y + TR - tY)_e + I + G = Y_a$, or

(6) $A + c (1 - t) Y_e + cTR_e + I + G = Y_a$.

Expressions (5) and (6) assume that only factor income, not transfer income, is subject to direct taxation. In fact, Canadian governments do levy direct taxes on some components of transfer income (for example, Old Age Security) as well as on factor income. If transfer income were fully subject to income tax, expression (6) would give way to

(6a) $A + c (1 - t [Y + TR]_e) + I + G = Y_a$.

But let us go back to using (6), and now, to simplify, we can lump together the 'autonomous' items A, cTR_e, I, and G ('autonomous' because we are not trying to explain them) in a new symbol H; then

(7) $H + c (1 - t) Y_e = Y_a$.

We also are going to continue to assume that expected income in each period is equal to the actual income from the previous period:

(8) $Y_e = Y_{a-1}$.

Over a number of periods, whatever level of income we start from, we eventually reach the equilibrium level of income, as we saw in the previous chapters. When this happens, expectations about income will be fulfilled; expected income will turn out to be actual income and will re-create itself the next period, so

(9) $Y_e = Y_a$, and thus, from (7),

(10) $H = Y_a (1 - c[1 - t])$, or

(11) $Y_a = H / (1 - c[1 - t])$, or

(12) $Y_a = H$ times $1 / (1 - c[1 - t])$,

and

(13) $\Delta Y = \Delta H$ times $1 / (1 - c[1 - t])$.

In words, the change in the equilibrium level of factor income (ΔY) that results from a given change in the autonomous components of expenditure (ΔH) is given by a multiplier that is no longer $1/(1 - c)$ but rather the smaller quantity $1/(1 - c[1 - t])$.

Thus by adding G to C and I, we have changed not only the level of demand but also the slope of the consumption function on the 45° line diagram. The slope, measured relative to Y, is flatter now: it is c (1 - t) now, not just c. Putting this another way, in the presence of government, the marginal propensity to consume out of additional factor income is lower, because some of the additional income will be taxed away.

One complication with which we have not dealt is the possibility that certain transfers, such as employment insurance (EI) and welfare, may be related to household factor income in a negative way - i.e., they tend to be higher when Y is lower. For example, when unemployment is high, and factor income is depressed, EI benefits and welfare payments tend to be high. It would not be difficult to build this relationship into our expression, but it would take us deeper than space allows.

In any case, let us summarize the effects when government makes a fiscal policy decision. First, what happens to the equilibrium level of income if G increases? Since this is equivalent to any other increase in autonomous spending, it increases GDP by a multiplied amount, though the size of the multiplier is reduced because of taxes. Using GDP as interchangeable with AD or Y, and following (13),

(14) $\Delta GDP = \Delta G$ times $1/(1 - c[1 - t])$.

Second, what happens if transfers increase instead? We do not get the same result; even though the full amount of the increase is added to disposable income, only part of it will be consumed (how much depends on the marginal propensity to consume); households will plan to save the rest. Therefore the final increase in GDE and GDP will be smaller than if the government had spent the money on goods and services itself.

(15) $\Delta GDP = c\Delta TR$ times $1/(1 - c[1 - t])$.

Third, what happens if direct taxes (T) increase? This is like a negative change in transfers, because it reduces disposable income, and households will react by altering both their consumption and their saving. Consumption will fall by a proportion c of the increase in taxes.

Using (4) again, because we cannot any longer assume a fixed tax rate, we find that

(4) $A + c (Y + TR - T)_e + I + G = Y_a$, so

(16) $A + cY_e + cTR_e - cT_e + I + G = Y_a$

Substituting H for the autonomous items as above,

(17) $H - cT_e + c(Y)_e = Y_a$ so, when $Y_e = Y_a$ at equilibrium,

(18) $H - cT = Y_a (1 - c)$ and

(19) $Y_a = (H - cT) (1/[1 - c])$, so

(20) $\Delta Y = \Delta(H - cT) (1/1 - c)$

The multiplier is back to its first incarnation, $1/(1 - c)$, but the influence of a change in T is, like that of a change in TR, moderated by multiplying it by c.

If what we are talking about is a change in the tax rate t, this changes the slope of the consumption function, which is c(1–t); see the discussion after expression (13).

To work out the change in the equilibrium level of income when the tax rate changes, in terms of the algebra, we could take expression (12):

(12) $Y_a = H \times 1 / (1 - c[1 - t])$

and solve it twice, once for the first value of t and once for the second value.

In any case, the important thing is to recognize that governments influence aggregate demand through three distinct channels: their own outlays on goods and services (G), their transfers to households, enterprises and non-residents (TR), and their taxes on households, enterprises, and non-residents (T). While the effect of an alteration in G is analogous to that of any other shift in autonomous outlays, a change in transfers or direct taxes does not alter GDP directly but rather influences it by its effect on the private sector's disposable

Chart 13. Federal government revenues and outlays, 1979–97

% of GDP

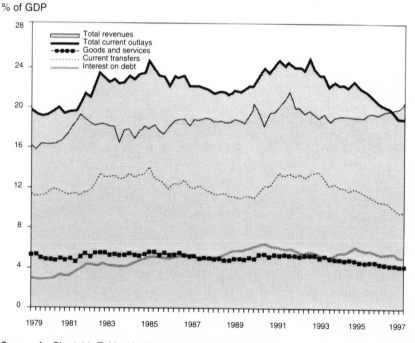

Source: As Chart 11, Table 10; data plotted quarterly (SAAR).

income, thus affecting the latter's capability both to save and to consume. (The effect on AD of a change in indirect taxes is different from the effect of a change in direct taxes; it is equivalent to that of a negative change in G because it comes through from the expenditure side.)

Recent Federal and Provincial Trends

Charts 13 and 14 show, for the federal and provincial levels of government, and in quarterly detail, recent trends in spending and revenue relative to the size of GDP. Since certain transfer programs (employment insurance, welfare) are very sensitive to employment trends, and since the general costs of government and programs such as education and health do not diminish when the economy falls into recession, government outlays rise sharply relative to GDP at such times (1982, 1990–1) and during the subsequent recoveries. The charts also make it clear, however, that both levels of government have initiated major spending reductions in the 1990s, so that, despite the economy's somewhat sluggish expansion, their finances had come into rough balance by 1997 and were heading into overall surplus. Chapter 9 discusses fiscal policy and debt management policy at greater length and, at the end, relevant economic indicators.

Chart 14. Provincial governments' revenues and outlays, 1979–97

% of GDP

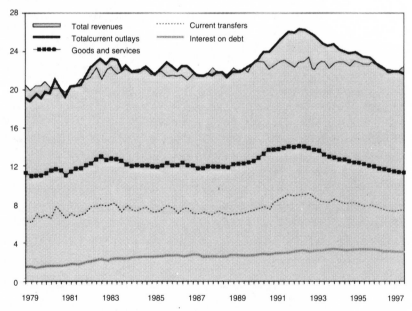

Source: As Chart 11, Table 11; data plotted quarterly (SAAR).

5

The Bank of Canada and the Deposit-Taking Institutions

Managing the Economy

In most countries, the central bank's assignment is to keep inflation low. In practice, however, this means that it has a much bigger responsibility as well – namely, to manage aggregate demand as a whole. While governments substantially affect private behaviour through their taxation and transfer policies, these are unwieldy instruments for managing economic fluctuations, since they are normally set just once a year. For practical purposes, the Bank of Canada, exercising subtle but pervasive control over aggregate demand through its influence on interest rates and exchange rates, governs Canada's economic engine.

The Bank of Canada and the Federal Government

The Bank of Canada was set up by the government in 1934, to act as its financial agent and to manage the country's money. Its board of directors is appointed by the government, but responsibility for policy and operations rests with the governor, who is named by the board, with cabinet approval, for a renewable seven-year term. In 1994, Governor Gordon Thiessen decided to manage through a governing council, consisting of himself and the five deputy governors. On a day-to-day basis, the Bank makes monetary policy independently of the government, but it was agreed in 1961 that in the event of a difference of opinion the government could issue a formal directive, and the governor, if unable to accept it, would resign. In 1994, when Governor Thiessen was appointed, he and the government agreed that the Bank would aim to manage inflation within a band of 1–3 per cent from 1995 to the end of 1998. They later extended the arrangement to 2001. The Bank and the government continue to search for a definition of 'price stability' that could form the basis of a more lasting inflation target.

In order to understand how monetary policy is made, we must first look at the Bank of Canada's balance sheet and those of the deposit-taking financial institutions.

The Bank of Canada's Balance Sheet

The Bank's principal liability (see Table 6) is its currency notes – for example, the five- and ten-dollar denominations in regular circulation. Its other liabilities are for the most part deposits by financial institutions, such as the chartered banks, that themselves take deposits from the public. To balance its liabilities, the Bank holds about $30 billion of assets, mostly securities issued by the federal government in the form of Treasury bills and bonds.

The Balance Sheets of the Commercial Deposit-Taking Institutions

The assets of the chartered banks and other deposit-takers (Table 7), such as the trust companies and credit unions, fall into two categories. 'Liquid assets' may include deposits at the Bank of Canada, holdings of currency, call and

TABLE 6
The Bank of Canada's balance sheet, end of December 1997

Asset/liability	$million	% of total
Government of Canada securities		
Treasury bills	14,065	44.3
Bonds	12,965	40.8
Other investments	4,719	14.9
Total assets	31,749	100.0
Notes in circulation	30,542	96.2
Deposits		
Government of Canada	41	0.1
Chartered banks	539	1.7
Other members of the Canadian Payments Association	25	0.1
Other	278	0.9
Other liabilities	324	1.0
Total Liabilities	31,749	100.0

Source: Bank of Canada Review (spring 1998), Table B1.

TABLE 7

The chartered banks' aggregate balance sheet, end of December 1997

Asset/liability	$million	% of total
Canadian-dollar liquid assets		
Bank of Canada deposits, notes, and coin	4,792	0.4
Treasury bills	21,473	1.6
Other Government of Canada securities	50,482	3.8
Call and short loans	1,115	0.1
Less liquid Canadian-dollar assets		
Personal loans	95,988	7.3
Business loans	200,996	15.2
Loans to governments	1,838	0.1
Residential mortgages	227,774	17.2
Non-residential mortgage loans	13,868	1.1
Leasing receivables	2,440	0.2
Provincial and corporate securities	54,452	4.1
Other Canadian-dollar assets	116,515	8.8
Total Canadian-dollar assets	772,433	58.5
Foreign-currency assets	548,638	41.5
Total assets	1,321,071	100.0
Canadian-dollar deposits		
Personal savings deposits	289,697	21.9
Non-personal term and notice deposits	141,323	10.7
Demand deposits	52,495	4.0
Government of Canada deposits	6,631	0.5
Other Canadian-dollar liabilities		
Bankers' acceptances	40,173	3.0
Subordinated debt	14,459	1.1
Other, including shareholders' equity	200,994	15.2
Total Canadian-dollar liabilities	745,772	56.5
Foreign-currency liabilities	575,299	43.5
Total liabilities	1,321,071	100.0

Source: Bank of Canada Review (spring 1998), Tables C3, C4.

short-term loans, and federal government securities and can be disposed of easily at any time without risk of significant loss. Less liquid assets typically earn higher rates of return but involve greater risk: these include loans to households, enterprises, and governments, as well as non–federal government bonds. In managing their portfolios, the banks continually balance safety and liquidity against risk and profitability.

The liabilities of these institutions consist mostly of households' and enterprises' deposits. Though some deposits do earn interest, they are held primarily to facilitate payments and/or to provide their owners with a secure store of value.

What Is Money?

'Money,' in Canada, refers to a specific set of financial assets. Though banknotes (such as twenty-dollar bills) and coins are the most familiar form of money, deposits at financial institutions are much more important. Table 8 lists the assets that are included in successively broader aggregates called M1, M2, M3, and M2 plus (M2+). It is evident from the table that M2 plus constitutes a close-to-comprehensive account of assets of stable nominal value, though some

TABLE 8
Measures of money (monetary aggregates), December 1997

Aggregate	Components ($million)	Total ($million)
Currency outside banks	28,638	
Personal chequing accounts at banks	12,103	
Current accounts at chartered banks	34,807	
Adjustments (NSA)	−881	
Float	1,454	
= M1		76,165
Chartered bank non-personal notice deposits	34,142	
Chartered bank personal savings deposits	290,232	
= M2		399,676
Non-personal term deposits and foreign currency deposits of residents (NSA)	151,530	
= M3		
		545,740
M2	545,740	
Trust and mortgage loan company deposits	48,834	
Credit union and caisse populaire deposits	91,003	
Life insurance company individual annuities (NSA)	44,225	
Personal deposits at government savings institutions (NSA)	6,977	
Money market mutual funds (NSA)	33,477	
Adjustments	542	
= M2+		624,547

Source: Bank of Canada Review (spring 1998), Table E1. NSA = not seasonally adjusted. SA components need not add up to SA totals.

observers might want to extend it to include individuals' holdings of Canada Savings Bonds (CSBs).

The term 'M1' refers to assets held primarily for holders' convenience in making payments. Certain other forms of money serve this purpose but are more useful to their owners as a safe and stable store of value. They may earn interest, but typically the rate is quite low; this is not the primary benefit that they offer. Assets such as term deposits, CSBs, and money market funds are often held by individuals in their Registered Retirement Savings Plans (RRSPs). Here they provide a buffer stock of liquidity if income should falter and earn a secure (nominal) rate of return over an extended period, thus reducing the volatility of the return on their owners' entire portfolios.

Credit is entirely different from money. A good example of credit is a loan. If you have a loan from a bank or trust company, you owe the institution, whereas if you have a deposit, the institution owes you. The Bank of Canada also each month publishes credit aggregates, which it constructs largely from the other side of these institutions' balance sheets. (In the case of business credit, however, a considerable part of the financing involved comes from non-deposit-taking financial institutions such as pension funds, or from individuals, through their purchase of instruments such as commercial paper, bankers' acceptances, bonds, and shares.) Table 9 shows the level of these aggregates at December 1997. Household Credit and Business Credit are the most timely and comprehensive measures available of the borrowing of households and businesses, respectively.[1]

A credit card is neither money nor credit; it simply assures a merchant that you are entitled to borrow from the issuer of the card. When you use it to pay for something, the issuer in effect extends you a loan. A debit card is different again; using it is like writing a cheque on a deposit and having it debited immediately from your account.

The Nightly Clearing

As we have seen, 'money' consists primarily of the liabilities of deposit-taking financial institutions. When you draw on your deposit at a bank, trust company, or credit union, by writing a cheque on your account, the recipient may deposit the cheque in his or her own account at another institution. At the end of the day it will be taken to a clearing house, and when all such claims have been presented, some of the institutions will turn out to be net debtors and others will be net creditors, and they must settle with each other overnight.

---

1   The money and credit aggregates are published by the Bank of Canada. See **Bank of Canada Weekly Financial Statistics** in chapter 11.

TABLE 9
Measures of credit (credit aggregates), December 1997

Aggregate	Components ($million)	Total ($million)
Consumer credit (SA)		138,652
At chartered banks (SA)	95,530	
At other institutions	43,122	
Residential mortgage credit (SA)		372,044
At chartered banks (SA)	226,303	
At other institutions	145,741	
Total household credit (SA)		510,696
Short-term business credit (SA)		238,911
Business loans at banks (SA)	119,300	
Business loans at other institutions	28,738	
Bankers' acceptances	41,927	
Banks' foreign currency loans to residents	29,740	
Commercial paper of non-financial corps.	18,575	
Other business credit		393,862
Non-residential mortgages	50,518	
Leasing receivables	13,394	
Bonds and debentures	124,528	
Equity and other	205,422	
Total business credit (SA)		632,774
Total household and business credit (SA)		1,143,470

Source: Bank of Canada Review (spring 1998), Table E2.

Canada's deposit-taking institutions are all members of the Canadian Payments Association, which operates the country's transfer and clearing system for funds. Since early 1999, transfers of large amounts, made electronically, have been settled with finality on an ongoing basis during the day, rather than at the end of the day, in what is called the Large Value Transfer System (LVTS). (Smaller items, such as personal cheques, continue to be cleared overnight, for retrospective settlement.) The institutions that participate in the LVTS settle the transfers between them by debiting or crediting the settlement balances that they are required to maintain on the books of the Bank of Canada.

Managing the Overnight Interest Rate

The Bank of Canada takes advantage of the institutions' need to maintain settlement balances with it in the way it operates monetary policy. Each morning, the Bank announces a band of fifty basis points (i.e., one-half per cent) at which it will lend or borrow overnight settlement balances to participating institutions. At the upper end of the band, called the Bank Rate, it will lend them (on a collateralized or secured basis) as much as they need to meet the day's requirement; at the bottom, it will take any excess balances off their hands. As a result, there is no need for them to pay higher rates, or accept lower rates, for overnight funds. This effectively confines the overnight rate within the band.

Over the course of a day, large transfers on behalf of customers continually add to or subtract from each institution's settlement balances. To ensure that they will have enough balances to meet their obligations, they trade securities with each other and with other market participants during the day, borrowing and lending at rates that reflect the relative tightness of funds. To encourage institutions to trade balances at a rate close to the centre of the band, the Bank of Canada will offer Special Purchase and Resale Agreements (SPRAs) or Sale and Repurchase Agreements (SRAs) to the primary dealers, a group of government securities dealers that trade actively in Government of Canada debt markets. If, during the morning, overnight funds are trading above the midpoint of the band, the Bank will offer to transact SPRAs – that is, it will lend funds to dealers at the midpoint of the band. Conversely, it will offer SRAs if funds are trading below the centre of the band. This supply or withdrawal of funds effectively provides settlement balances to the system, thus tending to encourage the overnight rate to trade around the midpoint of the band.

To maximize its profitability, each of the participating institutions wishes to obtain only enough settlement balances to meet its obligations but no more, ending up with a zero balance at the end of the day. The Bank of Canada, for its part, arranges that the overall supply of settlement balances for the system as a whole will also be zero. To do this, it takes advantage of its position as manager of the government's cash balances. In this role, it can transfer government deposits from itself to participating institutions, or vice versa, through two auctions, early and late in the day. When the size of the auctions goes up relative to the previous day, the stock of government deposits in the institutions' hands increases, and to transfer the funds the Bank credits their settlement balance accounts on its books. Conversely, by reducing the size of the auctions, the Bank would leave them with fewer government deposits than the day before and debit their settlement balance accounts accordingly. (The institutions can also trade balances with each other for a half-hour at the end of the day after the close of client business.) In practice, then, end-of-day deficits or surpluses in individual participating institutions' settlement balances at the Bank tend to be very small, and the institutions do not actually borrow or lend very much at the limits of the band.

Expectations and the Structure of Interest Rates

The overnight rate is the only interest rate that the Bank can fully control. Its $30 billion of assets is too small an amount to make it a dominant player in Canadian financial markets by the sheer force of its buying and selling. But it does have a huge effect on the entire structure of Canadian interest rates, primarily because it exerts a strong influence on other players' expectations.

An interest rate can be expressed as the ratio between the prices of a financial asset at two different dates. If you can buy a security today for $100 and redeem it a year later for $105, then you will earn 5 per cent on your investment. Another way you could invest for a year would be to buy a security maturing in six months and then buy another one with the proceeds of the first. If each costs $100, and pays back $102.46 at redemption, your rate of return for the year will still be 5 per cent, since the two rates will compound on each other (1.05 = 1.0246 x 1.0246).

At any one time, the structure of interest rates in financial markets ranges from an overnight rate (for the loan of money that is to be repaid the next day) to rates that apply to loans of thirty years and more. If, when the Bank of Canada sets the overnight rate for today, market participants expect it to set the same rate every night for the next week, then today's two-day, three-day, and even seven-day rates in the market will tend to be priced very close to the overnight rate, because other market participants will bid them up or down to make them so.[2] If market participants change their minds and come to expect the Bank to raise the overnight rate sometime during the coming week, the structure of rates will immediately reflect this: the rates for four-day, five-day, and longer loans will tend to rise above the overnight rate.

The Bank couples its manipulation of the overnight rate with press releases on its policies and intentions, which, being evaluated by market participants, gives it an impact on the whole structure of interest rates. While it has absolute control over the shortest-term (overnight) rate, it has somewhat less influence on three-month rates, one-year rates, and so on. These are sensitive to other forces, including the rates that are available in foreign financial markets, especially the United States. I will discuss these further in chapter 7.

---

2   To earn a rate of return over one week, you could achieve it with certainty by buying a one-week security or, with less certainty, by buying a succession of one-day, two-day, or similar securities. If everyone expects one-day rates to remain the same for the next week, the seven-day rate will tend to be close to the one-day rate, though how far above it or below it will depend on the degree of certainty with which expectations are held, as well as other factors.

The interest rates that are charged by the deposit-taking financial institutions to their customers, and interest rates on other classes of loans and securities, are closely correlated with the structure of interest rates that we have been examining.

Though our discussion has referred to nominal interest rates, the structure of expected real interest rates is involved as well, depending on what is happening to inflation expectations at the same time.[3] It is the structure of expected real interest rates that the Bank wishes to influence, because rising or falling real interest rates will reduce or increase, respectively, the desire of households and enterprises to invest in housing, machinery, buildings, and equipment. And through the multiplier, the change in the rate of investment will gradually shift the equilibrium level of income and aggregate demand. In turn, as we will see in chapter 7, this will affect the rate of inflation.

The Demand for Money

Why is money held? There are three motives for households and enterprises to hold real money balances as part of their asset portfolios: effecting transactions, precaution, and speculation. At any given time, the first two will be related to the level of aggregate demand: that is, the higher the level of spending on goods and services they expect to carry on, the greater the amount of money balances that they will want to hold to facilitate their transactions and reduce their risk of not being able to make payment. The third relates to nominal interest rates. If these are expected to rise in the near future, this anticipation implies that a capital loss will be imposed on holders of bonds.[4] To avoid the loss, some bondholders would wish to sell their bonds now and hold money instead (possibly planning to buy back the bonds when they have become cheaper). Interest rate expectations may be negatively related to the actual level of rates – i.e., if rates are perceived as 'low' (or 'high') now, most people may expect their next move to be up (or down). So on this argument the demand for money to be held for speculative reasons (not to be spent in the current period but simply to be held as a reserve) will be relatively high (low) when interest rates are low (high).

Let us consider then what happens to the demand for real money balances when the Bank of Canada is successful in raising nominal and real interest rates. As far as speculative demand is concerned, the effect of a rise in nominal rates depends on speculators' reactions. If it leads them to anticipate that rates

---

3   For an explanation of how real interest rates are computed, see p. 35 note 1.

4   A bond is a promise to pay a fixed series of interest payments and a fixed repayment of principal. In order to offer a higher (lower) rate of return to its buyer, its price must fall (rise).

Chart 15. M1 growth versus nominal GDP growth, 1980–97

Four-quarter
% change

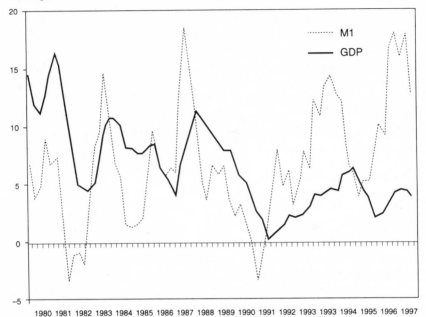

1980 1981 1982 1983 1984 1985 1986 1987 1988 1989 1990 1991 1992 1993 1993 1994 1995 1996 1997

Source: Statistics Canada, CANISM databases, Series B1627 and D14840.

will fall again in the near future (which means that bond prices will rise), then they will want to reduce their money balances in favour of bonds. As for transactions and precautionary motives, these will decrease as well for two reasons. First, higher real interest rates make money more expensive to hold (like any inventory); second and more important, the increase in interest rates will tend to reduce investment spending, which in turn, through the multiplier, will gradually lower the equilibrium level of income. This in turn is the chief influence on the transactions and precautionary motives for wanting to have money balances on hand. So, when interest rates rise, all three motives for holding money tend to be reduced, though the dynamics of this process (the timing and scale of the effects) tends to be quite complex.

Chart 15, which illustrates the relationship between the growth rates of M1 and GDP between 1980 and 1997, brings out a crucial point – growth in M1, while volatile, tends to anticipate GDP growth by about six months or so. This makes M1 growth a particularly useful economic indicator, and Statistics Canada includes it in the **Index of Leading Indicators** for just that reason.

In assessing the Bank of Canada's effectiveness, note carefully the huge role of private expectations and reactions. The Bank does not have full control over the processes by which these are formed, nor does it have full and immediate information about them. None the less, it has great power to influence aggregate demand, because it can be persistent in pursuing its objectives. It can keep shifting the overnight rate, for instance. But the paths of its influence are complex, and the time lags between its actions and their effects are long and variable. By the time the Bank gets clear evidence that its efforts are bearing fruit, it may have overdone things. It therefore tends to move the overnight rate slowly and cautiously, watching and waiting to assess reaction before embarking on another step.

The Supply of Money

The discussion in the preceding paragraphs has focused on the demand to hold money. What determines the amount available – the supply side? The Bank of Canada does, but in a relatively passive way.

Until 1992, the chartered banks were legally required to hold specific reserves of cash and other liquid assets in proportion to their deposits. To control the volume of bank deposits (and thus essentially the size of the money stock), the Bank of Canada could manipulate the supply of reserves, somewhat as it now controls the stock of overnight clearing balances.

These days, deposit-taking financial institutions, though no longer constrained by legal requirements, still manage their overnight balances very carefully relative to their deposit liabilities. The Bank of Canada, in the process of managing the overnight rate, thus still effectively controls the size of the country's stock of money. But the Bank has in the meantime abandoned its earlier practice of setting explicit targets for the growth rates of the monetary aggregates in favour of managing 'monetary conditions' – a combination of real interest rates and real exchange rates. I'll discuss them in chapter 7. In the Bank's view, monetary conditions, as opposed to money, have clearer linkages to aggregate demand and thus are more useful in managing inflation. Inflation is certainly a 'monetary' process, and the Bank understands that fact very well. However, the Bank now uses the level and growth rates of the monetary aggregates primarily as a source of information about future trends in aggregate demand and inflationary pressures, rather than as operational targets.

6

Canada's International Relationships

Canadians interact with non-residents, as they do with each other, by buying and selling goods and services, by borrowing and lending (i.e., acquiring financial assets from each other), and by making and receiving transfers. However, in the last decade, dealings with foreigners have become vastly more sizeable than ever before (Chart 16).

Statistics Canada reports on Canadians' economic relationships with non-residents in the **National Income and Expenditure Accounts**, Canada's Balance of International Payments (see **Balance of Payments**), and **Canada's International Investment Position**, all components of the SNA (described below in Chapter 11). It reports trade in physical goods in great detail in Canadian International Merchandise Trade (see **Merchandise Trade**).

Balance of Payments

The **Balance of Payments** (see Table 10) has three main components. The Current Account summarizes the flows of goods and services, investment income, and current transfers between Canadian residents and non-residents, while the Capital and Financial Accounts summarize cross-border changes in the ownership of financial assets between quarters or year's ends. More specifically, the Financial Account tracks cross-border financial transactions, whereas the Capital Account summarizes asset revaluations resulting, for example, from exchange-rate changes or write-offs. The Current Account is always equal to the sum of the Capital and Financial Accounts, albeit with the opposite sign, because all flows that are not matched by an opposite flow must establish or extinguish a claim. For example, if Canadians import more goods and services than they export, they also acquire an obligation to pay for the difference. That obligation would show up as a positive entry in the Financial

Chart 16. Exports and imports as proportion of GDE, 1980–97

% of GDE

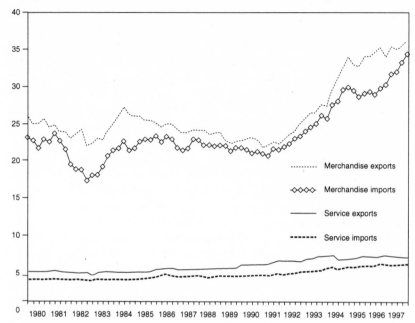

- - - - - - - - Merchandise exports

◇◇◇◇ Merchandise imports

——— Service exports

- - - - - - Service imports

Source: Statistics Canada, *National Income and Expenditure Accounts*, #13-001-XPB (fourth quarter, 1997), Table 2.

Account. There is a convention that Current Account receipts (for example, from exports) are shown with a positive sign, while Current Account payments have a negative sign, so if Canada imports more goods and services than it exports, this would contribute to a deficit on the Current Account. The Capital and Financial Accounts treat an increase in Canada's foreign liabilities (for example, when non-residents acquire Canadian financial assets) as positive, while an increase in Canada's financial assets abroad is negative (it represents an outflow of funds).

A Current Account deficit has to be financed by a financial or capital surplus – i.e., non-residents must be acquiring more Canadian financial assets than Canadians are acquiring financial assets abroad. However, persuading foreigners to acquire these assets may require a rise in the rate of return that is offered in Canadian financial markets. Portfolio management is a global business, and acquisition and divestiture of foreign securities by global fund managers have become routine. Fund managers can be persuaded to increase their

Canadian assets relative to those in other countries only if they expect that doing so will net them a higher rate of return, or a lessening in their overall risk, or both. If fund managers are to keep acquiring Canadian financial assets, short-term interest rates in Canada may have to rise higher and higher relative to those in other countries. But this is not necessarily the case. The required capital inflows might come in without such an increase if, for instance, perceived entrepreneurial opportunities in Canada were great enough to encourage strong inflows of direct investment. If that were the case, non-residents would still be attracted by high expected rates of return relative to risk, not in the financial markets as such, but rather by the opportunity to acquire controlling interests in Canadian enterprises. However, if Canada were unable to offer either one or the other of these sorts of opportunity, it would be unable to finance a continuing current account deficit except by selling assets.

Both current and financial cross-border transactions typically involve two stages. First, the transactor acquires foreign currency, and second, he or she uses it to purchase foreign goods and services or financial assets. Cross-border trading in financial assets is much heavier than trading in physical goods and services, because transactions and information costs are much lower relative to the value being traded. Foreign exchange markets, where currencies are traded, experience the highest volumes of all, because they are involved in both types of transaction.

Canada's International Investment Position (Table 11) summarizes Canada's assets abroad and non-residents' Canadian assets at the end of each year. Over the years, Canada has typically been a net exporter of goods and a net importer of services, and over time the sum of the two has been in deficit. This situation has forced the country to attract continuing net inflows of capital, largely through three mechanisms: foreign direct investment, reinvestment by non-residents of their earnings from Canadian enterprises, and non-residents' purchases of Canadian bonds. The last item, in particular, has gradually exacerbated the very problem that gave rise to it, since the resulting interest payments to foreigners have contributed massively to a growing deficit on investment income and thus on the Current Account itself. Though Canada has generated more than enough earnings from its foreign borrowing to service its foreign interest obligations, Table 11 makes it clear that Canada owes far more to foreigners than they owe to it.

Exchange Rates and Foreign Trade

There are two important definitions of the currency exchange rate between one country and another – nominal and real. The most familiar is the nominal

TABLE 10
Canada's Balance of International Payments ($million), 1997

	Receipts	Payments	Balance
Current Account			
Merchandise (i.e., goods)	301,601	278,237	23,363
Non-merchandise			
Services			
Travel	12,368	15,601	–3,232
Freight, shipping	8,330	12,393	–4,063
Commercial services	19,726	21,456	–1,730
Government services	957	755	202
Investment Income			
Direct investment	11,823	17,524	–5,701
Portfolio investment	3,422	29,207	–25,785
Other investment	12,847	13,212	–365
Current transfers			
Private	2,124	1,848	276
Official	2,439	2,390	49
Total Current Account	375,637	392,623	–16,986
Capital Account			7,601
Financial Account			
Decrease in foreign assets of Canadian residents			
Direct investment			–17,926
Portfolio investment			–11,400
Short-term investments			–27,385
International reserves			3,388
Increase in Canadian assets of non-residents			
Direct investment			11,421
Portfolio investment			21,027
Short-term investments			33,906
Total Capital and Financial Account, Net Flows			20,632
Statistical discrepancy			–3,646

Source: Statistics Canada, *Canada's Balance of International Payments*, #67-001-XPB, (fourth quarter 1997).
Note: A minus sign denotes an outflow of capital resulting from an increase in claims on non-residents or a decrease in liabilities to non-residents.

exchange rate – the price of a unit of domestic currency in terms of a foreign currency (for example, one Canadian dollar may cost U.S.$0.75), though professional currency traders often quote it the other way (one U.S. dollar costs

TABLE 11
Canada's International Investment Position, end of 1997

Asset/liability	$million
Canadian Assets Abroad	
Direct investment in foreign enterprises	193,674
Portfolio holdings of foreign bonds	27,505
Portfolio holdings of foreign stocks	83,962
Canada's reserves of foreign currencies	25,704
Loans and allowances	50,300
Deposits	100,478
Other claims on non-residents	68,167
Total	549,789
Canadian Liabilities Abroad	
Foreign direct investment in Canada	187,586
Foreign-portfolio holdings of Canadian bonds	373,180
Foreign-portfolio holdings of Canadian stocks	50,579
Loans to Canadians by non-residents	49,623
Canadian money-market instruments	43,820
Foreign deposits in Canadian financial institutions	165,558
Other Canadian liabilities to non-residents	184,404
Total	889,192
Net International Investment Position	−339,403

Source: Statistics Canada, Canada's International Investment Position, 1997, #67-202-XPB.

Can.$1.3333). Economists also refer to 'purchasing power parity' (PPP) between two countries – the ratio of the foreign price level to the domestic price level. The real exchange rate is the ratio of the nominal rate to PPP.

Why is PPP important? If borders are open to trade, and if it costs more to buy a good in one country than another, traders will tend to buy it in the cheaper country and sell it in the dearer one. Of course, the comparison has two components – prices in domestic currencies and the nominal exchange rate. For example, if a trader may buy a ton of steel for Can.$50 in Canada or for U.S.$40 in the United States, the steel is cheaper in Canada if the nominal exchange rate is below 1.25 (i.e., a Canadian dollar costs less than U.S.$1.25). The real exchange rate, which takes into account both these components, is thus a more meaningful measure of a country's competitiveness than the nominal exchange rate alone. However, not all goods and services are easily traded across international borders. So economists often calculate PPP by comparing price indexes that are composed only of the prices of tradeable goods and services, weighted by their relative contribution to the trade of the two countries involved. Published estimates of PPP vary considerably, because their constructors may differ on which goods and services to include, whether to use weights of the current year or of a base year, how to weight exports versus imports, and the base year to choose.

Even the most appropriate measure of PPP does not determine anything, in and of itself. But when we divide the nominal exchange rate by PPP, we get the real exchange rate, and this (if properly constructed for its purpose) is the most useful single index of one country's competitiveness with another.

Factors Influencing Aggregate Real Exports and Imports

Macro-economics provides a 'great simplification' about exports and imports, as it does about consumption and investment. In one sentence: a country's real exports of goods and services are affected positively by the size of foreign aggregate demand and negatively by real exchange rates.

The first part of this statement is quite straightforward: at a given time, exporters will tend to have won a certain share in foreign markets and therefore, other things being equal, will make larger exports if foreign aggregate demand grows. But the influence of real exchange rates is a little more complex to explain. Remember that a real exchange rate can vary either because one country's price level changes relative to the other's or because their nominal exchange rate changes. Suppose country A experiences high inflation, while country B does not. Then A's price level will rise relative to that of country B. If the nominal exchange rate does not change, A's real exchange rate with B will rise. (See the definition above.) Now A's exports have become more expensive for purchasers in B. As a result, A's exports are likely to win a smaller share of B's demand than before. Contrariwise, if the real exchange rate falls – because A's price level falls relative to B's, or because the nominal exchange rate declines, or both – A's exports will become cheaper for B, and A will tend to win a larger share of B's aggregate demand. If one country had a higher rate of inflation, but its nominal exchange rate fell by enough to offset this fact, then the real exchange rate between them would remain unchanged, and the countries' relative competitiveness would not be affected.

We can explain real imports of goods and services in a comparable way to real exports, except that demand for them is sensitive not to foreign but to domestic demand, and they are positively, not negatively, affected by the real exchange rate. That is, when A's domestic price level rises relative to B's price level, if the nominal exchange rate remains the same, A's real exchange rate will rise, making imports less expensive in A relative to domestically produced goods and services, thus tending to raise the import share of the domestic market.

Economic Indicators to Watch

Daily or weekly
Canadian–U.S. nominal exchange rate
Canada's G-10 exchange rate

Monthly
Merchandise Trade

Quarterly
Canada's International Investment Position
Current account balance
Investment income flows
Terms of trade

Here, as in many other areas, indicators tend to be volatile in the short term. Individual commodities' trade patterns can fluctuate sharply as a result of strikes and other interruptions to normal flows. Exchange rates too are potentially volatile, because managers in both financial and non-financial enterprises are often prepared to shift assets quickly from one currency to another when their perceptions of risk or reward change, since transactions costs in currency and financial markets are very low. It is therefore useful to form a preliminary, general view of what to expect and continually to test it against emerging data. For example, if one anticipates strength in domestic demand, surging imports will tend to confirm it. If real exchange rates fall and remain low for a time, one would expect a gradual strengthening of the real trade balance (real exports minus real imports) in response. If the merchandise terms of trade (the ratio of export prices to import prices) improve, they may be signalling stronger corporate profits, especially in trade-sensitive industries.

For the reasons noted, trends in real exchange rates are much more important than trends in nominal exchange rates, though they are not published by the official statistical agencies. (The International Monetary Fund's semi-annual *World Economic Outlook*, published in April and October, provides valuable commentary on these and other indicators of international competitiveness.)

Since exports and imports of goods and services each account for close to 40 per cent of Canada's GDP (Chart 16), and about four-fifths of this trade is with the United States, it is evident that Canada's economy is strongly dependent on that of its southern neighbour. The linkage of the two economies through financial markets is much more pervasive, however, since, as noted above, corporate managers routinely shift funds back and forth to take advantage of even slight cross-border differences in expected risk-adjusted rates of return.

As I show in the next chapter, the Bank of Canada emphasizes the role of exchange rates in its management of the overall trend of aggregate demand (and thus inflation). But exchange rates are not fully manageable by central banks. In fact the Bank is careful to say that it does not target the Canadian–U.S. nominal exchange rate at any given time. It does trade in the exchange markets regularly in the course of managing the government's foreign exchange reserves but does not intend these transactions to signal its views one way or another. From time to time, however, if it perceives excessive market volatility, it may offer to trade for its own account at a certain rate – a signal intended to calm and moderate fluctuations.

7

Monetary Policy

So far I have referred little to the price level (that is, the overall price index for the goods and services included in GDP). Households, enterprises, and governments base their decisions mostly on their perceptions of 'real,' not nominal values, and above I have ignored the price level as such, except as it influences PPP. But the central bank works very hard to manage the rate of change of the price level – that is, the rate of inflation – and we need to know why and how.

In chapters 3 and 6, I did discuss three 'prices' that affect real aggregate demand – namely, the real wage and the real interest rate (which influence investment) and the real exchange rate (which affects exports and imports). But it turns out that the overall price level has an independent influence on real aggregate demand (AD) as well – because of money.

If we graphed the relationship between the price level and real aggregate demand at a point of time, we would find that it sloped downward to the right. That is, a rise in the price level would typically reduce the volume of goods and services demanded. But we have to take two factors as given, in order to make that statement – the nominal money supply (or money stock) and the state of inflation expectations.

Why would a rise in the price level reduce AD? Basically, because it would reduce the real value (the purchasing power) of the nominal money stock. Each dollar would buy fewer goods and services. Since households and enterprises hold money primarily to facilitate the real expenditures that they expect to make, they would respond to the rise in the price level by attempting to rebuild the real value of their money balances, in order to carry out conveniently their intended spending. How would they do this? Typically, by reducing their holdings of other financial assets, such as bonds. But this would tend to reduce the prices of these assets, which would raise nominal and real interest rates. Over time, the higher level of real interest rates would tend to reduce investment spending and, through the multiplier, the level of AD.

But this chain of events is not complete. The fall in AD would reduce the level of real money that transactors feel they need to hold, since they are now planning to spend less. So households and enterprises would find that they have somewhat greater real money balances than they need. This situation would reverse the chain (interest rates would fall) and the process would continue, back and forth, until the demand for real money balances has finally become equal to the reduced supply. Note carefully: we assume the nominal money stock to be fixed.

We thus end up with the price level higher but AD lower, so that the nominal money stock is once again just as much as people want to hold; but we have not explained why the price level rose in the first place or, indeed, why it moves at all. Before dealing with that, however, let us look at inflation expectations (IEs).

The Importance of Inflation Expectations

How do IEs influence AD? – primarily through their effect on real interest rates. Taking the level of nominal interest rates as given, if IEs rise for some reason, then the effective level of real interest rates would drop, since real interest rates are equal to nominal rates minus IEs for the relevant future period. In turn, if maintained, the lower level of real interest rates would tend to stimulate investment and thus, through the multiplier, AD as a whole.

Since IEs can influence AD in this way, we need to know how they are formed. An influential school of economists argues that they must be formed 'rationally,' since errors in forecasting inflation can be very costly, and it is certainly worthwhile to acquire information on the subject. (To be 'rational' in this context is to act on the basis of as much information as it appears to be cost-effective to acquire.) However, empirical work suggests that IEs, or at least those that are significant in financial markets, are actually largely formed 'adaptively,' in reaction to recent experience, whether or not this implies fully rational behaviour.

As an example, suppose that actual inflation used to be 5 per cent but has moved towards 4 per cent over the last year or so. If IEs are adaptive, the consensus forecast of inflation will have started at or near 5 per cent and begun to move towards 4 per cent as well, with some lag. If inflation then picks up, the consensus inflation forecast will gradually shift back upward too.[1]

---

1   This does not mean that everyone forms IEs in the same way, but financial market prices tend to move as if they did. Since financial markets do appear to 'back-cast' inflation in this way to some degree, anyone who could forecast inflation better than that might be able to outperform them.

The Bank of Canada has recently argued that its commitment since 1991 to a specific inflation target range has helped to focus IEs on that range, so that even if inflation did escape from the range in the future, market participants would resist shifting their IEs in response. But the credibility of the target range has hardly yet been put to the test.

How Is the Price Level Determined?

The price level is not just a random number. The best way to explain how it is set is to start by discussing how we determine its rate of change – that is, the rate of inflation. To do this, we need two new concepts – potential output and the output gap.

Potential output (PO) we can define as the level of output that the economy could produce at a given time, using the available factors of production (labour with its skills, capital with its embedded technology) just fully enough that inflation would tend neither to rise nor to fall. The output gap is the difference between AD and PO. If AD is above PO, the output gap is positive – the economy is experiencing very heavy demand – and inflation will tend to accelerate. If AD is below PO, the output gap is negative and inflation will tend to slow.

Chart 17 illustrates AD and PO between 1980 and 1997. We measure AD, as usual, by the level of real GDE each quarter. Statistics Canada does not measure PO, but the Bank of Canada does unofficially, and it kindly supplied the data for the chart. The gap, as noted above, is the difference between AD and PO. Chart 18, which covers the same period, illustrates the relationship between the output gap, measured as a percentage of PO, and inflation, as measured by the implicit GDE deflator.

On What Does Potential Output Depend?

Roughly speaking, the level of PO depends on the size and skills of the labour force and the size and technologies of the installed stock of capital. The size of the labour force in turn depends not only on the size of the population of working age but also on the willingness of individuals to seek work, while the size of the capital stock depends not only on the rate of investment over time but also the rate at which the installed stock depreciates. Unfortunately, the stock of embedded skills and technologies is much easier to talk about than to measure.

So why does inflation rise and fall in response to the size of the output gap? Suppose that inflation is established and proceeding at, for example, 6 per cent

Chart 17. Real GDP and potential output, 1980–97

Millions of 1992 dollars (SAAR)

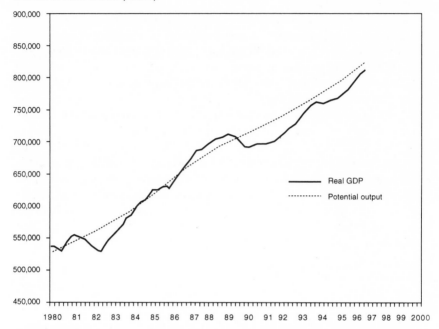

Source: Statistics Canada, CANSIM database, series 14840; Bank of Canada, private communication.

a year. Producers of goods and services have to decide what prices to charge for their products, and since they seem to form their IEs primarily from their recent experience, they will tend to set their product prices at a rate consistent with those IEs. The more aggressive, confident producers will try to raise prices by more than 6 per cent, while those with older, less attractive products may try to maintain their market share by raising prices by less than 6 per cent.

If AD exceeded PO, the more aggressive producers and distributors would find their price-hike gambits unusually successful, because there would be little competition for the available business. Inflation would thus begin to average higher than 6 per cent. In contrast, if the output gap were negative, competition for the available business would be fierce. More producers and merchants would be forced to reduce their price demands (and their profit margins) to stay competitive, and thus the rate of inflation would fall.

If inflation did rise or fall for any significant length of time, IEs would begin to rise or fall adaptively as well. In turn, a new band for price-setting would emerge. So, as long as the output gap was either positive or negative, the rate of inflation would tend to continue rising or falling, because nothing would stop it from doing so.

Though StatsCan does not publish a formal estimate of Canada's potential output, one can use various techniques to estimate it. A growing labour force, a growing stock of capital, and continuing upgrades in skills and technology all raise PO. In contrast, when investment spending declines, or the rate of growth of the labour force drops, or the rate of technological adaptation falls, then the growth of potential slows down.

Looking at Chart 18, we see that while the output gap is related to changes in the inflation rate, the correspondence is by no means exact. Many factors influence inflation, and the Bank of Canada acknowledges that it is difficult at any given time to know just how high PO, and thus the output gap, might be (and therefore how much upward or downward pressure there is on inflation).

Despite this uncertainty, the Bank places great weight on PO, and when it perceives that the output gap is likely to become positive, it will tend to expect

Chart 18. Inflation and the output gap, 1980–97

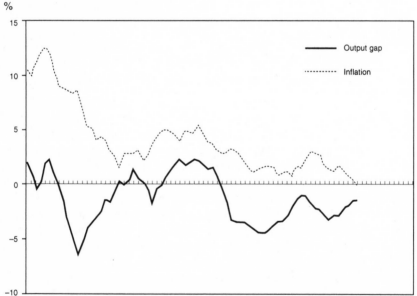

Source: Statistics Canada, CANSIM database, series 15612; Bank of Canada, private communication. Inflation is measured by rate of change of implicit GDP deflator.

inflation to rise, and if this rise would take inflation above its target range, it will seriously consider taking action to prevent it.

How the Bank of Canada Influences the Rate of Inflation

Since early 1996, the Bank has publicly defined a fifty-basis-point range for the overnight interest rate. As described in chapter 5, it enforces the overnight rate primarily by shifting government deposits between itself and the chartered banks, thus augmenting or reducing their overnight clearing settlement balances. This leads the banks to bid higher or lower overnight interest rates for these balances in order to restore their desired operating levels. When the Bank wishes to change the rate, it announces the decision through a press release, and market participants instantly 'get the message.'

The rate for overnight funds anchors the short-term end of the structure of nominal interest rates. Market expectations about the Bank of Canada's future activities extend this influence towards the longer-term end of the nominal yield structure. Of course, the level and shape of the yield curve do not respond only to the Bank's actions. They also reflect the transactions (and indirectly the expectations) of all the other lenders and borrowers, at home and abroad, that participate in Canada's securities markets. The structure of U.S. interest rates is crucial.

Given inflation expectations, the nominal interest rate structure determines the structure of real interest rates as well. (That is, the nominal interest rate for any given term is the relevant real interest rate plus whatever risk premium is currently required to reflect inflation expectations.)

As we saw in chapter 3, the structure of real interest rates has a direct, but lagged impact on investment in housing, fixed capital, and inventories. A rise tends to discourage and reduce these components of aggregate demand.

The structure of nominal interest rates, relative to those abroad, also influences money flows into the Canadian dollar, as investors are attracted to or away from Canadian relative to foreign securities. The capital flows that are attracted or repelled by Canada's interest rate structure will influence the nominal exchange rate and therefore, given the price level (and foreign price levels), the real exchange rate. As we saw in chapter 6, a rising real exchange rate tends to weaken exports and strengthen imports, which worsens the overall trade balance and weakens AD. Of course, as we know, the multiplier mechanism amplifies these influences.

Through these channels the central bank thus exerts a significant, though delayed influence on aggregate demand. The Bank of Canada recognizes that it exerts power not through real short-term interest rates alone but through the combination of real interest rates and real exchange rates, which it calls 'mon-

Chart 19. Monetary Conditions Index, 1987–97

Percentage

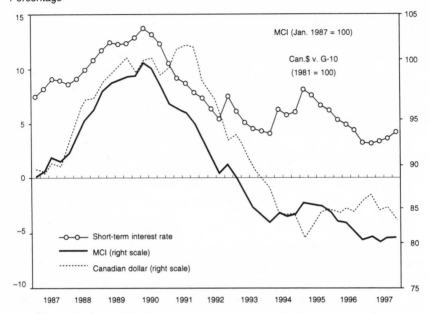

Source: Bank of Canada; Statistics Canada, CANSIM database, series B113858, B113929, and B3418. Chart illustrates index and series on which it is based: three-month prime corporate paper rate and index of Canadian dollar against trade-weighted average of currencies of Canada's G-10 trading partners.

etary conditions.' To inform public discussion, the Bank each month publishes a **Monetary Conditions Index**, or **MCI** (see Chart 19), which it bases on a weighted average of a nominal three-month interest rate and a weighted average of Canada's nominal exchange rates with its nine major trading partners.[2]

However, expectations in foreign exchange markets are critical here. If domestic and foreign investors become pessimistic about the Canadian dollar and expect it to depreciate over the period during which they plan to hold a Canadian security, they will demand a higher yield from it (combining its

2   The MCI should in principle average real interest rates and real exchange rates together, but the use of nominal values is considered to be easier for the public to grasp. Since the MCI is a device for communicating the Bank's stance to the public, this consideration was a key factor in its design. See the discussion of the MCI in chapter 11.

income yield and any expectation of capital gain or loss in Canadian-dollar terms) to compensate them for the expected currency depreciation. The Bank's own interest-rate moves may generate such speculation. For example, a rise in the Bank's overnight rate range may generate market expectations that the Bank intends to bring about an appreciation of the currency. The shift in exchange-rate expectations would reduce the required return on Canadian-dollar securities in Canadian-dollar terms, because investors would expect to earn some part of their total return through the currency's rise. Investors would tend to shift out of foreign securities to buy Canadian-dollar securities, placing upward pressure on the Canadian-dollar nominal exchange rate (an example of self-fulfilling expectations). This pressure would further tighten monetary conditions. If this end was not the Bank's intention, it would have to find a way to ease monetary conditions again, without exciting too much speculation in the other direction.

Since exchange-rate expectations are volatile, manipulating monetary conditions can be tricky. Not only may currency speculators place an unwanted interpretation on the Bank's moves, they are also very sensitive to political issues (such as Quebec separation) beyond the central bank's control. For this reason, estimating the amount of capital flows (in or out) that will be generated in response to a given shift in the Canadian overnight rate (up or down) is not straightforward.

Largely because of the unpredictable and somewhat volatile nature of exchange-rate expectations in world financial markets, the Bank disclaims responsibility or even desire to maintain any particular level of the nominal exchange rate. When it feels that the combination of the exchange rate and the short-term interest rates – i.e., monetary conditions – is inappropriate, it shifts the overnight rate range to achieve a better combination and often accompanies this action with a statement intended to help financial-market participants understand its intentions.

In deciding what monetary conditions are appropriate, the Bank of Canada first chooses a target for the medium- to long-run average inflation rate – that is, the rate of change of the price level. As noted above, the inflation rate will tend to change over time at a rate which depends on the size of the output gap. The Bank compares its inflation target to the actual inflation rate (more precisely, to the inflation rate that it expects in the medium term if it does nothing) to decide how large an output gap to create.

The Bank compares this desired output gap to the actual output gap (more precisely, to the output gap that it would expect in the medium term if it did nothing) to decide how much it should change monetary conditions. It then takes steps to bring about the desired monetary conditions.

Complications in Monetary Management

The Bank's forecasters must exercise a great deal of judgment, because many elements of the economy are difficult to forecast and are vulnerable to unpredictable shifts and shocks. The lags between a change in monetary conditions and the resulting shifts in aggregate demand, in the output gap, and in inflation are variable and imprecise, though they are generally considered to have their greatest weight about six to eight quarters ahead.

Managing monetary conditions can be likened to lion-taming. Armed only with the ability to control the overnight rate and some signalling devices (such as its semi-annual *Monetary Policy Report*, the governor's speeches, and press releases), and with whatever degree of credibility its actions have brought about, the Bank must confront and attempt to influence real interest rates and expectations about inflation and exchange rates. These factors are simultaneously being influenced by the actions of Canadian politicians and by other developments around the world. Even the Bank's own actions can be misinterpreted, with potentially damaging consequences.

Because the Bank must always stand ready to respond to changing market expectations aroused by forces beyond its control or its ability to predict, it must from time to time take actions that run counter to its medium-term intentions, in order to deal with short-term difficulties.

For all these reasons, the Bank considers itself always to be approximating to the desired path, continually resetting its tactics, accepting setbacks along the way, and trying to overcome them. In practice, it tends to make small, persistent changes in the overnight rate, rather than large ones. It strongly disavows any intention of managing the nominal exchange rate. Under Governor Thiessen it has adopted a policy of 'transparency,' meaning that it takes great pains to explain its views and its purposes as clearly as possible. However, on occasion, it must move boldly and even dramatically, in order to counter changing market expectations and influence monetary conditions in the direction that it wants to bring about.

Is Managing Inflation the Same as Managing the Price Level?

We have now discussed how the rate of inflation is managed in Canada. Is this equivalent to managing the price level itself? The question comes down to this: if inflation goes outside its target range for a time, so that the price level goes above or below what had been anticipated, will the central bank attempt to restore it by pushing inflation outside the target range in the other direction for a time, or will it simply allow 'bygones to be bygones,' by bringing the inflation rate back into the target range but no further?

Certainly, the price level will not manage itself. Since it interacts with the size of the money stock, the Bank of Canada carefully monitors the monetary aggregates in deciding how to manage inflation. But Bank publications suggest that it is inflation, not the price level as such, that is the object of policy.

The Federal Reserve System and the Relationship between Canadian and American Interest Rates

In the United States, the Federal Reserve System (the 'Fed'), under its board of governors, operates monetary policy (see description of the system below, p. 162). Though it has no formal inflation target, in practice it appears to have been managing inflation in much the same range as the Bank of Canada. Given that the U.S. economy is much less 'open' than Canada's (exports and imports account for about 14 per cent of U.S. real GDP, compared to some 36 per cent of Canada's), the role of the real interest rate is far more important relative to that of real exchange rates in U.S. monetary conditions. The 'Fed' operates policy primarily through its control over the Federal Funds rate, which is analogous to Canada's overnight rate. The board of governors is dominated by its chairman (currently Alan Greenspan), who is appointed for a seven-year term by the U.S. president.

Though the Fed must report semi-annually to Congress, it manages monetary conditions as it considers appropriate. Because the U.S. economy is the largest in the world and contains the most active financial markets, its interest rates tend to set the pace for those in other economies, especially smaller economies whose fortunes are tightly tied to it, such as Canada's. Though the Bank of Canada dominates the short-term end of the Canadian yield curve, as the Fed dominates the short-term end of the U.S. curve, longer-term rates in Canada are strongly dominated by their counterparts in U.S. financial markets. Long-term rates in the two countries differ primarily because of differences in risks perceived by investors, including credit concerns and expectations about exchange rates and inflation.

Interpreting Economic Indicators in the Presence of the Central Bank

It should be clear by now that the economic indicators report on an economy strongly influenced by policy feedback. Like a private observer, the central bank watches the indicators, assessing them against its own expectations, but, unlike the private observer, when it perceives that they suggest that inflation may begin to depart from its target range, it takes action by shifting monetary conditions. Because of the considerable lags between policy actions and the private sector's responses, the central bank 'tries out' its policies by running them through multiple computer simulations and continually validates them in practice by comparing the economic indicators with what they had anticipated. If the indicators remain consistent with expectations, the central bank can continue on the same policy path. If not, it must evaluate the message – how reliable is the indicator? is its signal confirmed by other indicators? – before altering policy.

Many economic indicators are measured with error, especially at the time of first release, when the surveys on which they are based may be less reliable. Partly for this reason, the Bank of Canada is loath to make large, dramatic changes in the overnight rate, preferring instead to make small changes, accompanied by rhetorical devices such as speeches and press releases to prepare market participants for further moves.

8

The Labour Market

The Key Issue: Stability of the Real Wage

The labour market – where the price of labour is determined – is central to the economy. The key question is this: when the demand for labour changes, does the real wage (the nominal rate of compensation, divided by the price level) tend to respond strongly? Or can firms hire essentially as much or as little labour as they want at a given time without having to adjust their real wage offer very much? (In this discussion, the 'real wage' stands for the real value of the total compensation package, including supplementary benefits, offered by an employer.)

Individuals have to choose whether to offer themselves for work or to 'choose leisure' instead. 'Classical' economists argued that workers, needing to work, would respond to changes in the demand for their services primarily by adjusting the real wage. For example, if the demand for labour dropped, they would quickly reprice themselves downward in order to stay employed: 'leisure' in effect could mean starvation. Chart 20(A) illustrates this type of world. Here the supply curve of labour is vertical, so that we have an economy that is essentially always pretty close to 'full employment,' because the real wage takes the strain, rising and falling to keep the labour force fully employed. In other words, everyone who can work is available to do so and usually does work, but not necessarily at a rate of pay that he or she would like.

Chart 20B offers a modified version of this theory. Here the quantity of labour supplied is somewhat responsive to changes in the real wage that is offered. At least some workers can be enticed to work (or to work longer hours) only by a high real wage. If the demand for labour shifts upward, more

Chart 20. Labour-supply alternatives

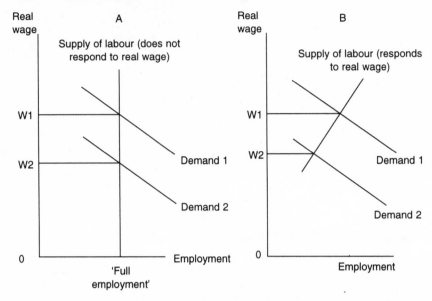

workers or worker-hours will come forward to satisfy it, as long as the real wage rises.

A third sort of case arises if the real wage is inflexible. Suppose that employers and employees are very slow in adjusting the real wage in response to changing circumstances. (If one group is prepared to be flexible, the other may not be.) In this case, if demand for labour falls, the real wage will not – and unemployment will rise instead. However, if demand for labour rises, people will be put back to work, but there will be no effect, or only a slight effect, on the real wage. This is sometimes called a 'Keynesian' case, illustrated by a more-or-less horizontal supply curve for labour.[1] Though it caricatures Keynes's own views of the labour market, it does reflect the reality that unemployment does exist and varies with the state of demand. Keynes actually noted that nominal wages resisted downward adjustment in Britain in the 1930s. Nominal-wage inflexibility was even worse than real-wage inflexibility, because to the extent that product prices were falling, real wages were actually rising, making labour even more expensive to hire and putting more people out of work.

---

1   John Maynard Keynes (1883–1946), influential Cambridge economist, a prime mover in the development of modern macro-economic theory and policy.

The Canadian Evidence: Relative Real-Wage Stability

Unfortunately for the 'classical' view, workers' average real compensation is astonishingly inflexible in Canada. It rises at a rate that is much more stable than either employment or output. Chart 21 illustrates the major fluctuations in Canada's real GDP from 1980 to 1997. There was a recession bottoming in 1981–2, a boom in the late 1980s, and another recession bottoming in 1990–1. The chart shows the fluctuations in output, employment, and real compensation around their trends. Clearly, the greatest fluctuations were in output – when it rose or fell, the number of jobs instantly responded, but not so dramatically as output itself. Only a secondary, much less significant response was made by a rise or fall in the average real rate of compensation. In fact in 1991–2, when output and employment were falling relative to trend, the real wage went in the other direction! (The bracketed figures show the average rate of growth of each series between 1980 and 1997.)

Chart 21. Read GDP, employment, and real labour compensation relative to trend, 1980–97

% of trend value

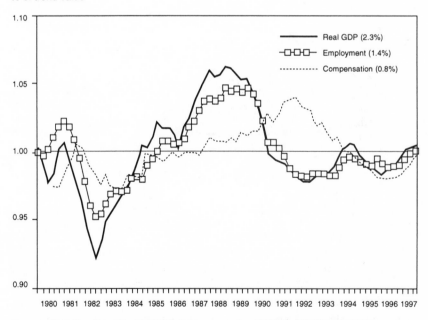

Source: Statistics Canada, CANSIM database, series D14872, D14896, D15612, and D980595.

Not only employment fluctuates in response to output shifts: the rate of labour-market participation does as well (Chart 22). The size of the working-age population grows relatively steadily, whereas the size of the labour force (those who indicate that they either have a job or are available for work) fluctuates along with employment – workforce participation varies with the cycle. When demand weakens, some people appear to become 'discouraged' by the difficulty of getting jobs and actually drop out of the labour force. In the face of substantial fluctuations in aggregate demand, employment and labour-force participation take most of the stress in the labour market; the real wage hardly adjusts at all. So, though it might seem that workers could avoid major spells of unemployment by being flexible in their demands for compensation when the demand for labour rises and falls, as in the classical model, this does not seem to be how things really work.

Chart 22. Growth of working-age population, labour force, employment, and real GDP, 1981–97

% growth year over year

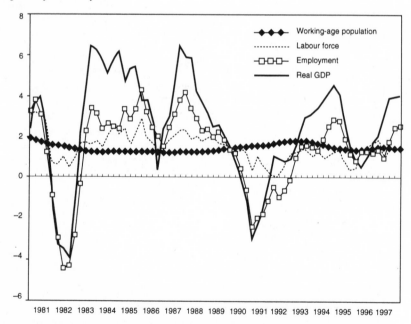

Source: Statistics Canada, CANSIM database, series D14872, D980000, D980562, and D980595.

Real Wage Growth Reflects Long-Run Productivity Trends

Chart 23 shows that the rate of change of compensation in nominal terms is strongly correlated with the rate of inflation, usually being about 1 to 2 per cent above it. The growth of the 'real wage,' which is the difference between them, tends to be relatively steady, in the range of 1 per cent a year (it actually averaged about 0.8 per cent a year between 1980 and 1997). In fact, real wage behaviour appears to be dominated not by fluctuations in the demand for labour over the business cycle but by long-run productivity growth. In other words, workers and firms appear to behave as if they agreed that real compensation should increase at a relatively steady rate, reflecting the long-term rate of increase in real output per worker.

Shares of the Income Pie

Labour income is of course only one component of net domestic income (NDI). Of the other three major elements – corporate profits, proprietors' income, and investment income – the first are the most sensitive to the demand cycle. Chart 24 illustrates the fluctuations of labour income, profits, and investment income as percentages of total NDI between 1980 and 1997. (The share of proprietors' income was relatively stable and is not shown.) The profit share and the labour share both fluctuated sharply during the period, largely at each other's expense. On average, labour's share is far larger than that of profits (labour income has averaged about 71 per cent of NDI since 1980, and profits, about 12 per cent). Since the labour share rises sharply in recessions (for example, 1982, 1991) and falls sharply in booms, the result is a huge proportional swing in profits. In other words, though the rate of increase of real wages remains relatively steady during the business cycle, labour income and profit shares do not.

Investment income has averaged about 10 per cent of NDI since 1980, in the context of two developments that are unusual by historical standards. First, government debt grew much faster than GDP through this period. Second, real as well as nominal interest rates have been relatively high for most of the period. The combination of rapidly rising debt with relatively high rates of interest escalated the investment-income share to a range that is high by historical standards. The great loser from this is of course the taxpayer, who has to service the debt (and currently has been enlisted in a major struggle to reduce it as well).

But the situation is complex, because the household sector has also been the chief buyer of the government's debt and in this role has evidently benefited from the situation. The enterprise sector is the one that has become unreserv-

Chart 23. Inflation versus growth of labour compensation

% change, year over year

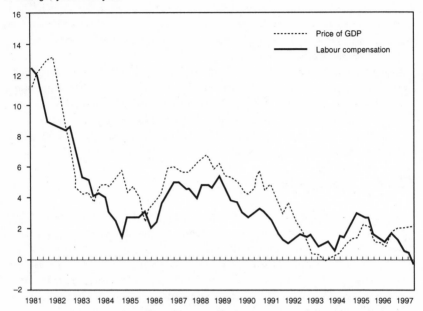

Sources: Statistics Canada, CANSIM database, series D14896, D15612, and D980595.

edly worse off, because it is not only a taxpayer but also a net borrower. The increase in real interest rates brought about by growing government debt has forced enterprises to pay the high rates as well. (Foreign investors for their part were made better off, because they were net buyers of Canadian government debt throughout the period.) Now that governments are moving into surplus, and interest rates have fallen, the investment-income share of NDI is falling as well. Not unexpectedly, while this is proving a major boon to the enterprise sector and its shareholders, it is a mixed blessing to households.

How NDI Behaves over the Business Cycle

Here is a brief summary of income-side events during a typical 'business cycle.' Suppose that aggregate demand begins to fall for some reason. GDP and NDI both drop. In the short run, since firms have relatively fixed costs, especially for labour and interest on debt, corporate profits drop sharply. Enterprises respond not by cutting the real wage that they offer but by letting people

Chart 24. Shares of the income pie

% of net domestic income   % of net domestic income

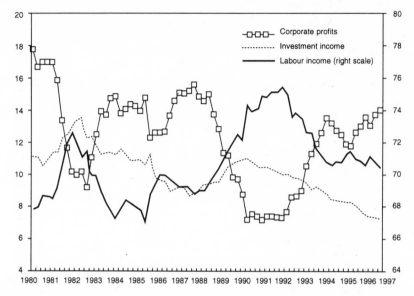

Sources: Statistics Canada, CANSIM database, series D14805, D14806, D14808, and D14812.

go. As employment drops, some workers begin to drop out of the labour force, but not as quickly as jobs disappear, so the unemployment rate goes up. Labour income none the less rises to its highest share of NDI during these recessionary episodes. The reason for this is that the real wage remains relatively stable and employment drops less rapidly than output. In other words, corporate profits take most of the strain of response to falling demand, which permits the labour share (of the shrinking pie) to rise.

When aggregate demand picks up again, things work more or less in reverse. Corporate profits rise very quickly, being highly sensitive to the increase in output. More weakly than output, employment begins to pick up; the real wage does not rise much if at all. Labour-force growth speeds up in response to better perceived employment opportunities. This reaction tends to keep the unemployment rate from dropping rapidly, but it does gradually fall.

Implications for corporate planners are clear: the inflexibility of labour-market conditions makes profitability extremely sensitive to fluctuations in demand. Firms thus do well to plan for an entire business cycle at a time, forming strategies to deal with contingencies and unexpected shocks and, even more important, anticipating monetary and fiscal policy measures that may from time to time impose severe trading conditions in the course of enforcing inflation or debt-management targets.

Though it is not easy to adopt this medium-term perspective, it is crucial to plan with the entire cycle in view. By the time a recession has become obvious, it is usually too late to take the most effective action.

Why Is the Real Wage So Unresponsive to Changing Demand Conditions?

Let us suppose that the unemployment rate is high. Suppose as well that there is a group of unemployed workers who are desperate for work and willing to work for less than the going real wage. In other words, they would accept whatever nominal or real wage it takes to get a job. Unfortunately for them, from the employer's point of view, this tack may not be as easy to implement as it sounds. To reduce the real wage for the new hire may mean doing the same for all the current workers as well. In other words, there is typically a pretty fixed proportionality between all the job rates in the firm, depending on the skill and experience required and so on. But the current workers will strongly resist a cut in their real wages, since they are still employed. And if there is a union involved, it can be even more difficult to change the wage offer, not only because of its organized resistance but also because the current collective bargaining agreement may have a number of years to run. In the meantime, neither the firm nor an individual worker can really make a deal to work for less. So, even though there may be plenty of people willing and able to do the job for less, they may not be able to make themselves attractive enough to hire, at least not in the short run – and the short run can be pretty long.

Sometimes there can be a problem in the labour market because the two sides have different inflation expectations (IEs). Suppose that firms observe that the prices of their products are falling and that this perception leads them to reduce their IEs for future periods. From their point of view, it would be reasonable to offer a lower nominal wage. But the workers' own IEs probably reflect a very broad range of consumer prices – for example, those measured by the **Consumer Price Index** (**CPI**). If the CPI as a whole has continued to rise, then the workers will not be willing to settle for a lower nominal wage, because it will imply a lower real wage for them than it does to the firm. The difference in the two sides' IEs can lead to bargaining problems. If they cannot agree, layoffs can result.

For these reasons and more, what we actually observe in the labour market is a high degree of 'stickiness' in the real wage and thus considerable volatility in the level of employment. But Chart 23 shows that the stability of the real wage does not come about because the nominal wage and the price level are stable. Far from it. We have had dramatic swings in price inflation, but they have been matched very closely by the swings in wage inflation. So it appears that workers have not been able or willing to use the real wage as a tool to stay employed in bad times.

Some people might describe this inability of workers to bargain wages down as a pathological situation, because of the severity of the costs imposed on those who are unemployed against their will. You might think that it should be relatively easy for people to remedy the situation simply by offering to work for less. But the evidence shows that this has not worked out very successfully in practice. In fact, far from going down, the real wage went up in the recession year 1991. What seems to have happened was that the drop in inflation that year caught bargainers by surprise. Wage agreements set in previous periods (reflecting relatively high IEs) were still in effect, producing high nominal-wage gains and therefore much higher real-wage increases than had been anticipated by either side.

In the end, we have to agree that Keynes put his finger on a central fact of life – namely, that wages are 'sticky' and that unemployment can be highly persistent. Keynes in the 1930s argued that in such circumstances it would be appropriate to increase government spending or transfers, or cut taxes, to stimulate aggregate demand. Some of his followers in the 1950s and 1960s, dismissing inflation as a minor issue, encouraged policy-makers to stimulate aggregate demand even beyond potential, which resulted in major inflation in the 1970s and 1980s. In turn, central banks reacted by bringing about major output gaps to reduce inflation, even though they recognized that this would generate unemployment. Policy-makers today appear to have few effective means for reducing the volatility of employment, except to the extent that they can achieve a more stable growth rate for output itself.

This discussion does not deal with the many causes of secular unemployment – that which arises for reasons unrelated to the demand cycle as such. Issues such as skill obsolescence, long distances between labour markets, and the generosity of transfers to the unemployed are major micro-economic concerns but cannot be dealt with here.

Economic Indicators to Watch

Average Hourly Earnings (**AHE**) (monthly)
Employment
Help-Wanted Index (monthly)
Labour-force participation rate
Ratio of employment to population

9

Fiscal Policy and Management of Public Debt

On one level, the aim of fiscal policy is simply to finance a desired level of government services prudently. But as we saw in chapter 4, there is much more to it. Federal and provincial governments' fiscal policies – their decisions about the size of current and capital outlays on goods and services, transfers, and taxes – affect profoundly the incentives that underlie private demand. However, if the Bank of Canada thought that these fiscal policies might push inflation outside the target range, it would certainly tighten monetary conditions, which would feed back in turn on governments' own revenues and outlays, including their debt-service costs.

Since both fiscal and monetary policies significantly affect the level of GDP, they must be coordinated. As we have seen, each works very differently on the economy. Fiscal restraint depresses private outlays either by raising tax rates or by cutting government expenditures or transfers. As a result, with less spending in view, private appetites for borrowing may fall, and the government's own need to borrow would decline too if the result were a rise in revenues relative to outlays. The economy's need for non-residents' saving would thus be reduced, which would allow Canadian long-term interest rates to fall relative to those abroad. Conversely, as we saw in chapter 7, monetary restraint works in part by raising interest rates. While both methods of restraint will slow the economy and reduce inflationary pressure, the pattern of influence is obviously different.

In recent years, the federal government has assigned the major responsibility for managing aggregate demand to monetary policy. It has defined the task as that of achieving and then maintaining a path for real GDP that would, as it grows over time, be consistent with a low inflation target. Thus the Bank of Canada must try to manage aggregate demand at close to potential output, keeping the output gap small except when inflation needs to be nudged back into its target range for whatever reason. Federal (and provincial) fiscal policies have therefore been free to concentrate on other goals, with primary focus in recent years on reducing public debt.

Federal and provincial decisions on fiscal policy are generally announced once a year in formal budgets. The federal government goes first, in February or March; the provinces, which take account of the federal fiscal framework, are usually finished by June. Though many budget measures go into effect overnight, others (such as changes to payroll-tax withholding rates) must wait until midyear at the earliest. (In contrast, monetary policy shifts can be made and implemented immediately.)

In all cases, however, the private sector's response takes a good deal of time – even years – to develop fully. Some responses are more rapid than others, and analysis of the lags is a very difficult part of forecasting. But the effects of policies and of the interactions among them make sense only in the light of the private sector's response lags. The problem is complicated by the unpredictability of private expectations, which determine the lags and the strength of responses and are themselves influenced by almost anything you can name.

In any case, policy-makers now understand that the effects of their policies take years to work through, and they have come to see their annual budgets as incremental contributions to an evolving stance. Forecasters must thus try to grasp the long-term objectives of federal and provincial policies if they are fully to understand the reasons why particular measures are introduced at a particular time.

National Finances and the Public Debt

The Canadian government's fiscal year runs from 1 April to 31 March (the U.S. government's runs from 1 October to 30 September), and it is thus important to distinguish fiscal from calendar years.

The Public Accounts of Canada (see Table 12) are the form in which the federal government reports its operations to Parliament each year. They represent a long-established method of accounting for revenues and expenditures. Most items of revenue and expenditure are 'budgetary,' but there are a certain number of 'non-budgetary' items, including loans to crown corporations and transactions in special funds such as the Canada Pension Plan Account and the superannuation accounts for civil servants. The total of budgetary and non-budgetary items generates the government's 'net financial position' to which is added the result of operations in foreign exchange. (The Bank of Canada buys and

TABLE 12
Federal Budgetary Accounts, 1996-7

Revenue/expenditure	$million
A Budgetary revenues	140,896
Personal income tax	63,282
Corporate income tax	17,020
Employment-insurance premium revenues	19,816
Excise taxes and duties	29,098
Non-tax revenues	8,833
B Program spending	104,820
Major transfers to persons	33,986
Major transfers to other levels of government	22,564
Direct program spending	48,270
C Operating surplus or deficit (A-B)	36,076
D Public debt charges	44,973
E Budgetary expenditures (B+D)	149,793
F Budgetary deficit (A-E) (equals increase in net public debt)	-8,897
G Non-budgetary transactions	10,162
H Financial surplus (ex foreign exchange) (F+G)	1,265
J Net foreign exchange sold	-7,759
K Increase in cash balances	811
L Total borrowing (K-H-J)	7,305

Source: Finance Canada, Fiscal Reference Tables (Oct. 1997), Tables 1, 3, 7, 15.

sells foreign currencies for the government's Exchange Fund Account; when it sells them, it acquires Canadian dollars for the government, which action, by adding to its cash balances, reduces the need for domestic financing.)

The government thus meets its net Canadian-dollar financing requirement either by issuing securities or by reducing its cash balances. The Bank of Canada manages the cash and debt operations for the government. The accounts are estimated monthly, on a cash basis – that is, revenues and expenditures are recorded when they are received or spent.

An alternative presentation of the government's accounts is the National Accounts version. This system, following the conventions of the System of National Accounts (SNA), records all items of revenue and expenditure on an accrual basis, whether or not cash is actually received or paid out at the time. It classifies revenues into direct taxes, indirect taxes, other current transfers from persons (miscellaneous taxes and premiums), investment income, and sales of goods and services.

It classifies current outlays into expenditures on goods and services, current transfers to the other three sectors of the economy, and interest on the public debt. The difference between revenues and current outlays is government net saving. Adding capital consumption allowances (CCA) gives gross government saving, which is available to finance government investment (outlays on capital) and capital transfers. The SNA is estimated quarterly.

The Federal Deficit or Surplus

The deficit or surplus can be defined in at least four ways. The best-known is the budgetary version (see Table 12) — the balance of budgetary revenues and budgetary expenditures, omitting major non-budgetary items. Also widely used is the difference between revenues and current and capital outlays in the National Accounts. Third, and more inclusive, is the net Canadian-dollar financial requirement – the amount of money the government borrows, plus any rundown in its cash balances. In addition, some economists calculate a cyclically adjusted deficit – an estimate of what the deficit would be if fiscal measures were unchanged but the economy were operating at full employment.[1]

The Public Debt

The government's deficits have added up cumulatively over the years to the public debt (see Table 13). The gross debt – the sum of all the government's outstanding obligations – is largely in the form of marketable securities (bills and bonds) in outside hands, but a substantial portion is held by internal accounts, mainly government employees' superannuation funds. By subtracting the government's financial assets from the gross debt, we arrive at the net debt. (Non-financial assets, such as crown lands, canals, harbours, roads, buildings, and equipment, are charged off to budgetary expenditure when they are acquired and are carried on the government's Statement of Assets and Liabilities at a total value of $1.) The increase or decrease in the net debt in each period is equal to the budgetary deficit or surplus for that period. The outstanding stock of net public debt at the end of fiscal 1996–7 was $583 billion, or about 65 per cent of GDP (see Chart 25). Interest on the public debt has now become the largest single component of federal spending.

The ratio of the public debt to the GDP rose continuously between 1975 and 1996, leading to increasing concern by lenders that ultimately the government

---

1   Economists argue about the rate of unemployment that is implied by the phrase 'full employment.' However, since the Bank of Canada is now managing the economy with reference to its concept of potential output, not full employment as such, the 'full employment' deficit or surplus is not as frequently referred to as before.

TABLE 13
Federal debt, end of fiscal 1996–7

Liability/asset	$million
Interest-bearing debt	600,557
Unmatured debt	476,852
Marketable bonds	305,579
Treasury bills	135,400
Canada Savings Bonds	33,493
Other	2,380
Debt held in public-sector accounts	123,705
Other liabilities	40,100
Gross public debt	640,657
Net financial assets	57,471
Net public debt	583,186

Source: Finance Canada, *Fiscal Reference Tables* (Oct. 1997), Tables 14 and 16.

Chart 25. Ratio of federal net debt to GDP, 1980–97

% of GDP

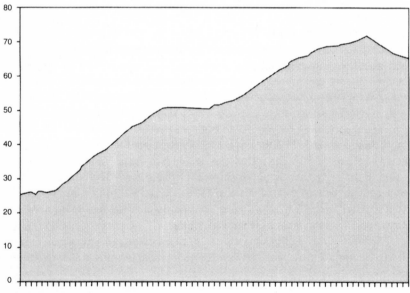

1980 1981 1982 983 1984 1985 1986 1987 1988 1989 1990 1991 1992 1993 1994 1995 1996 1997

Source: Public Accounts of Canada; Statistics Canada.

might be unable or unwilling to service it, at least in terms of dollars of stable purchasing power. To the degree that such anxiety leads lenders to demand higher real interest rates, a vicious spiral can erupt. In such circumstances, if the government were to try to reduce interest rates – for example, by directing the central bank to ease monetary conditions, lenders' anticipation of the inflationary (and currency-depreciating) consequences would soon exact a heightened risk premium, leading nominal interest rates to rise, not fall. This credibility issue is at the heart of the debate about the prudence of persistent deficit financing.

But the size of the net debt in relation to GDP has itself become a major target of policy. Successive efforts to trim deficits had been relatively unsuccessful during the 1980s, largely because they were undertaken just when the Bank of Canada was aggressively fighting inflation. The latter policy required that a negative output gap be opened up and maintained for a considerable time; this in turn implied high unemployment, weak tax revenues, and, especially when employment insurance benefits and welfare programs were relatively generous, soaring costs for transfer programs (see Charts 13 and 14). The high nominal interest rates involved in the Bank's policy of restraint only exacerbated the servicing costs of the fast-rising debt.

Only when the Bank shifted to a stimulative policy in the early 1990s, the inflation battle won, did government finances begin to improve. By this time, however, both the federal and provincial levels of government had embarked on severe expenditure restraint; rising aggregate demand brought with it rapid growth in tax revenues; monetary stimulus came through lower short-term interest rates; and the result was a soaring improvement in public finances and finally the achievement of budgetary surpluses by most governments by 1997–8.

Despite this quick improvement, the burden of interest payments remained very heavy, severely constraining governments' fiscal flexibility. In the event of another recession, governments could afford to do little to assist private households. Some economists argue that Ottawa should aim for substantial annual budgetary surpluses for the next decade or more, in order to reduce the ratio of debt to GDP from its 1996 peak of 71 per cent to 40 per cent or even 20 per cent by 2010 or so. Such a policy would sharply reduce the interest cost of government, permitting tax rates gradually to fall or expenditure programs to become more generous again. Demographic factors form a major part of such considerations, since once the 'baby boomers' have begun to retire, from 2010 onward, the ratio of elderly to working-age Canadians is likely to grow quickly, placing the burden of income tax on a shrinking proportion of the population while increasing the costs of health care.

102 A Handbook of Economic Indicators

Sources of Relevant Information

See the monthly **Federal Government Fiscal Position** in chapter 11. A convenient source of information on the federal government's financial position is Table G1 in the quarterly *Bank of Canada Review*, which provides up-to-date and historical data on federal revenues and expenditures on the basis of both the Public Accounts and the National Accounts. Another valuable source of detailed information on federal and provincial revenue and expenditures is *The Finances of the Nation*, published annually by the Canadian Tax Foundation. Revenue and expenditure data on a budgetary basis for the individual provinces is conveniently brought together in Finance Canada's annual *Fiscal Reference Tables*, published in October.

10

Using the Indicators

Peering into the early years of the twenty-first century, one sees in North America and western Europe central bank–managed regimes engaged in maintaining the low-inflation environment established with difficulty during the 1980s and 1990s. Fiscal policies in these countries will probably continue to be broadly oriented to reducing the ratio of public debt to GDP, anticipating heavy demands on the social safety net as the baby boomers retire. Enterprises will continue incorporating new telecommunications-based technologies. Asia, eastern Europe, Latin America, the Middle East, and Africa, thirsty for development funding, will play increasingly by the rules of global finance, while struggling to acquire the physical infrastructures, educational attainments, and legal, financial, and accounting frameworks that will enable them to realize their potential economic growth. Reduction in environmental stress will become more central in governments' activities. The internet will encourage households, enterprises, and governments alike to forge new links – a bewildering spider's web, apparently gossamer but incredibly strong and flexible, settling lightly over the world.

Despite the novelty of these challenges, economic cycles in the major countries, including Canada, still follow a path around potential real GDP, managed more or less by a central bank whose aim is to maintain a low average rate of inflation in the medium term. In Canada's case, the central bank makes detailed projections of the economy in order to manage the output gap, as discussed in chapter 7, but shocks can disturb the gap by unpredictable amounts and for varying lengths of time. Supply shocks (weather- or catastrophe-related, for instance) can temporarily reduce the availability of major factors or raw materials, raising their prices relative to other goods and leading producers to try to substitute other inputs, at the cost of inevitable delays in delivery and higher costs. Demand shocks (for example, an upsurge in investment in response to a rapid change in technology) may also shift the outlook unexpectedly. Economic developments in other countries, whether or not they are direct trading partners of Canada, can generate trade shocks, affecting Canada's exports and imports through the terms of trade (the ratio of export prices to import prices), the volume of trade, or both.

In any case, the central bank, which will have embarked on a particular policy course after examining a range of possible scenarios, will often have to contend with events or factors not fully anticipated. In such situations it must first decide how it thinks the economy and inflation would develop if it did not change its own policies and then whether and how it should intervene to put aggregate demand back on a more appropriate path. An individual's successful forecasting then requires that he or she put himself or herself in the central bank's place and try to anticipate both its basic game plan and how it will react to shocks.

At the level of the economy as a whole, real labour compensation per worker grows at a very stable rate over time, as we saw in chapter 8. Enterprises appear to react to changes in the output gap primarily by altering the level of employment, rather than by increasing or reducing the real wage that they offer. The rate of growth of the real wage appears to reflect an implicit consensus of business and labour about the rate of growth of labour productivity over the medium term.

But firms are typically unable to counter the effects of a changing output gap on their profits simply by changing the level of employment. The amount of work that they offer tends to vary less than their output, for a number of reasons. Firms may under-react to a shift in demand until enough time has passed to clarify its extent. Then, too, they are typically reluctant, as a slowdown develops, to lay off individuals in whom they have a substantial training investment and equally reluctant, in an upturn, to add new full-time workers, who would require substantial training and commitment. In the meantime, the ongoing modernization and improvement of technology, embodied through constant investment in new equipment and structures and scrappage of obsolescent stock, keeps potential output increasing. It grows relatively steadily (see Chart 17), because the installed capital stock is large relative to the fluctuations in investment spending from year to year. Thus, another reason why employment is slow to turn up when demand for output increases is that firms can often get by for a time simply by using the growing capital stock and current employees more fully. For all these reasons, real labour income – the product of the real wage and employment – tends to be much more stable than real GDP. When real GDP alters, so does labour income, but by a smaller proportion, so that labour's share of GDP and NDI tends to rise during slowdowns and fall during expansions.

When the central bank is concerned about a potential increase in inflation relative to its target range, it pushes up the overnight rate, which tends to shift the entire structure of real interest rates upward and may raise real exchange rates as well. The tightening of monetary conditions shifts the economy towards a negative output gap by slowing the growth of real GDP. Corporate profits suffer doubly when this happens – labour's share of NDI tends to rise, as does the share of NDI earned in the form of interest, the latter not only because of higher real and nominal interest rates, but also because the volume of corporate debt tends to rise rapidly at such times. The profit share thus takes the entire strain and more, when total NDI begins to fall. Conversely, it rises dramatically when NDI turns upward.

The volatility of corporate profits is astonishing. Profit as a proportion of NDI fluctuated between 17 per cent in 1980 and only 7.3 per cent in 1991. It then recovered to 13.5 per cent of NDI by the first quarter of 1995, fell off to 11.8 per cent in the second quarter of 1996, and had rebounded to 14 per cent by the final quarter of 1997 (see Chart 24). In downturns, this sort of swing means that there is not enough profit to support all the firms that exist. So bankruptcies increase sharply in recessions, giving the firms whose finances and labour relations are most flexible a massive survival advantage. Conversely, in upturns, even mediocre firms can do well, but this phenomenon gradually attracts a large number of inexperienced new entrepreneurs, many of whom overestimate their probability of survival. The high profitability of operations in the early phase of an economic expansion tends to encourage firms to accept relatively high debt and lease obligations, which increases their vulnerability to the next downturn.

How can a business strategist deal with these characteristics of the economy? One clear message from macro-economics is the role of medium-term scenario analysis (for example, planning in a four- or five-year framework, giving serious consideration to alternatives formulated from assessing official strategies and possible shocks). Since it is far from possible to forecast accurately, the best approach is to enumerate the components of the story, subject them to separate assessment, then combine these insights into a watchful preparedness, above all looking beyond the immediate prospect to the medium term.

Despite the rapidity with which computing and telecommunications are changing trade patterns, central banks will continue to manage the major economies with stable, low inflation in view, fiscal policy is likely to focus on public-debt management for at least a decade, enterprises in every country will continue to embody rapid technological change, and most households will base consumption decisions on their perceptions of trends in their income and wealth.

Here is a possible checklist to use in formulating a medium-term view on the Canadian economy. One might begin by assessing prospects generally in the areas that contribute most to the world economy: the United States, western Europe, and Japan.

- For each area, what inflation trend do you expect the central bank(s) to aim at?
- Is inflation close to the desired level?
- Does it appear that the region is above or below its potential output at present?
- Form a judgment on the central bank's desired path for real output during the forecast period.
- In each region, is the ratio of public debt to GDP moving in the intended direction?
- In this light, to what degree are governments' fiscal actions likely to restrain or augment aggregate demand over the next few years?
- Will a rising ratio of debt to GDP put upward pressure on the region's real long-term interest rates, or is the opposite likely?
- Given this policy framework, what path may monetary conditions take in each area? (Whereas the Bank of Canada's monthly **Monetary Conditions Index** places a third of its weight on exchange rates and two-thirds on short-term interest rates, the U.S. Fed and the Bank of Japan, which do not publish a formal MCI, would use weights more like one-tenth to nine-tenths if they did; the new European central bank might do so on the order of one-fifth to four-fifths, reflecting the difference in these jurisdictions' respective openness to foreign trade.)
- Propose some possible paths for Canadian nominal and real interest rates, and the nominal and real exchange rate against the U.S. dollar, if central banks and governments carry out their intentions as you understand them.
- Given this policy setting, develop scenarios for the key components of Canadian aggregate demand and the key factor income shares (especially highly sensitive corporate profits).

Every component in an exercise of this sort is subject to considerable uncertainty. Try to focus on a relatively few scenarios. However, many components are interdependent: a development in one may imply complementary developments in others. Remember that monetary and fiscal authorities will probably throw their weight in such a way as to try to achieve medium-term policy goals for inflation targets or ratios of debt to GDP. This likelihood narrows the range of probable outcomes.

It is not particularly important, or even possible, to forecast accurately. Our grasp of what has been happening is at best fragmentary, and we are always vulnerable to surprises and shocks (ranging from political events such as assassinations to climatic or natural disasters). What is crucial is the exercise itself. Thinking through the issues will generate useful questions, will make clear the areas where you need better information, will alert you to concerns not being discussed in the media, will prepare you for possibly dramatic shifts in interest rates and/or exchange rates, will give you a framework within which to assess the implications of unexpected shocks, and will allow you to formulate plans of action in advance. The idea is to come up with a general view of the future that is broadly consistent with what we can know and that places your firm's (or for that matter your own) plans firmly in a structural context.

Obtaining Information on the Economy

The most useful single source of economic information for the businessperson is Statistics Canada's monthly *Canadian Economic Observer*, #11-010-XPB, which contains a written commentary (with a feature article) and a statistical summary. It includes some brief information on other G-7 economies as well. There may be more here than you can use. But an hour or so spent browsing through it, once a month, will help you to formulate a view. As well, the quarterly *Bank of Canada Review* provides useful articles on economic developments.

In my view, the best single journalistic source of information on international macro-economic developments and trends is the *Financial Times* of London, followed distantly by the *Wall Street Journal*. The International Monetary Fund (IMF) and the Organization for Economic Cooperation and Development (OECD) both publish semi-annual economic surveys which, though somewhat constrained by political correctness, provide a valuable window on experts' opinions about the forces driving world-wide economic developments.

The following chapters provide the website address for each of the major Canadian and U.S. indicators. The major Canadian chartered banks and some other financial institutions provide daily commentary on the economy through their websites; here are a few addresses to get started with (the list is neither complete nor intended as a recommendation): www.bmo.com/economic/econ.htm; www.cibc.com/products/economics/; www.royalbank.com/economics/index.html/; www.scotiabank.com/eccomm.htm/. The website of the Canadian government's Department of Finance, www.fin.gc.ca, has useful links to other sites, as does that of Statistics Canada, www.statcan.ca, and that of the Bank of Canada, www.bank-banque.canada.ca. A short list of useful U.S. websites is provided at the beginning of chapter 12.

11

The Canadian Indicators

You can easily get access to the major economic indicators for Canada and the United States through the internet. Each of the indicators listed in chapters 11 and 12 has a website address, and a further list of useful websites is provided in the next chapter. But a few warnings are in order. In particular, the first ('advance') releases of some indicators are based on limited data, sacrificing accuracy for timeliness. And even if the estimated level is fairly reliable at the time of first release, the size or direction of change from the previous period may not be. Even if the data are well measured at first release, the series itself may be volatile; in such cases, forecasters often average two or more months' values together in deciding what to make of the data. Charts, going back a year or more, can provide very useful perspective. Think of the indicators as pieces of a larger jigsaw puzzle. They should serve either to strengthen, or cast doubt on, a scenario that you have already constructed. Unfortunately, it is rarely possible to dismiss a scenario on the basis of a single piece of data; rather, over time, a sifting of the emerging data will lend greater weight to some hypotheses and less to others. For this reason, you may find it useful to develop a list of indicators to follow on a regular basis.

Professional forecasters have certain advantages; for one, they can feed the data into mathematically sophisticated models that can help them to draw conclusions that would not be obvious to observers with fewer resources. But the latter are not out of luck. They can obtain the views of many expert, well-resourced forecasters, including the Bank of Canada and the Federal Reserve Board, on the web and in print, practically free of charge. At the very least, you can compare and contrast such opinions with your own; but in the end you have to make your own decisions, and for this it is wise to maintain some first-hand acquaintance with the indicators themselves.

This chapter describes the indicators by frequency of publication: weekly, monthly, quarterly, and annually.

WEEKLY INDICATORS

Bank of Canada Weekly Financial Statistics

Key numbers: interest rates, exchange rates, **Monetary Conditions Index** (MCI), monetary aggregates
Reporting agency: Bank of Canada
Website: www.bank-banque-canada.ca
Usual timing: Friday afternoon (after 2:00 p.m.)
Reference period: Wednesday, two and nine days previous; monthly data are averages of Wednesdays
Revisions: frequent, but usually small

Description

The Bank of Canada's *Weekly Financial Statistics* (*WFS*) contains the latest value of the **Monetary Conditions Index** (MCI), which is the best single indicator of the Bank's policy stance. *WFS* also provides detailed information on the latest monthly levels of the monetary aggregates, the assets and liabilities of the chartered banks and other deposit-taking institutions, the structure of interest rates, the exchange rate of the Canadian dollar vis-à-vis other major currencies, and a record of recent public and private financing activity. You should read the MCI in the context of the governor's frequent speeches and the Bank's semi-annual *Monetary Policy Report* (issued in May and November), both available on the Bank's website. Taken together, they provide both an invaluable summary of the economic outlook and a succinct and revealing window into the Bank's assessment of economic conditions. Given the Bank's responsibility for managing the economy's path over time, they represent a 'must read' for anyone wishing to form an opinion on Canada's economic outlook. The quarterly *Bank of Canada Review*, excerpted on the website, is a good source of insightful articles and statistics on Canadian economic and financial conditions.

MONTHLY INDICATORS

Average Hourly Earnings (AHE)

Key numbers: average weekly earnings for all employers and for all industries, for hourly paid employees
Reporting agency and source publications: StatsCan, *Survey of Employment, Earnings, Payrolls and Hours*, #72-002-XPB; StatsCan *Daily*

Website: www.statcan.ca
Usual timing: last week of month (8:30 a.m.); release dates published a year in advance
Reference period: the second month before preliminary release, three months before 'revised' release
Revisions: one month; annual revision of SA and raw data, going back four years, with release of final December data

Description

Statistics Canada derives the data from a census of administrative records for large and complex establishments and from a sample of administrative records for smaller establishments. The census portion includes all establishments within enterprises that operate in more than one industry or in more than one province and that have approximately 300 or more employees. The administrative records used are the payroll-deduction forms submitted by employers to Revenue Canada. On these forms, employers report total employment and payroll as well as the pay period associated with their remittances.

In order to obtain estimates of variables not reported on the administrative forms, the Business Payroll Survey (BPS) directly surveys approximately 10,000 firms. This survey provides the basis for estimating the weekly component of payrolls reported for periods other than weekly, total paid hours, and allocation of total employment, hours, and earnings by category of employees. 'Employees' comprises full- and part-time and working owners, directors, and other officers of incorporated businesses but excludes owners and partners of unincorporated and professional practices, the self-employed, unpaid family workers, persons working outside Canada, military personnel, and casual workers. It also excludes those who did not receive any pay (for example, were on strike or unpaid holidays) during the survey's entire reference period – the last seven days of the month.

Employees are classified into three categories: those paid by the hour, those on salary (whose basic remuneration is a fixed amount for at least one week), and 'others' (paid principally by commissions, piece rates, mileage allowances, and so on).

Average hourly earnings (AHE) is a key measure of workers' earning power and is a weighted average of hourly paid workers' gross pay, including overtime and a portion of bonuses, commissions, and other types of special payments, before deductions for taxes and employee contributions to employment insurance (EI). The AHE series excludes supplementary payroll costs such as employers' contributions to EI, medical plans, and workers' compensation funds. The data appear for 281 sub-industries and special industry groupings (such as goods, services, and public administration) not including agriculture, fishing and trapping, private household services, religious organizations, and the military.

StatsCan also publishes a measure of Average Weekly Earnings (AWE) for the same industries, including all employee categories, not only hourly paid but also salaried workers and those paid by piece rates and commissions.

Average hourly and weekly earnings for each industry and province change from month to month because of alterations not only in wage rates but also in number of workers counted, hours worked, and mix of jobs among industries, provinces, and methods of remuneration. For this reason StatsCan publishes fixed-weight AHE and AWE indexes, which hold these elements constant. These indexes provide a better indicator of underlying trends in wage rates than the variable-weighted earnings series.

Significance and Limitations

These surveys provide the most timely series available on Canadian wages and are a major input into StatsCan's estimates of labour income. Each month, it prepares statistics from the two latest surveys. It classifies data for the most current month, based on a response rate of about 80 per cent, as preliminary. It also prepares revised estimates for the previous month, based on a higher rate of response (approximately 85 per cent). A major problem is lack of timeliness, since the full preliminary data appear three months after the month to which they refer. Also, the design of the surveys has changed over the years. Beginning in 1994, StatsCan began a multi-year survey redesign to improve the quality and consistency of estimates and to reduce the reporting burden on businesses. Each phase of the redesign corresponded to increased reliance on administrative records. Now completed, this gradual change increased the risk of discontinuities in the data series. As noted above, changes in AHE and AWE from month to month reflect differences not only in wage rates but also in the mix of jobs. The fixed-weight series is thus a more useful measure of pure wage change.

Building Permits

Key numbers: Value of building permits for single- and multi-family residential dwellings, Canadian total

Reporting agency and source publications: StatsCan, *Building Permits*, #64-001-XPB; StatsCan *Daily*

Website: www.statcan.ca
Usual timing: first week of the month
Reference period: second month before the release
Revisions: annual publication in March revises the data for three years back.

Significance

StatsCan prepares a monthly survey of municipalities' awards of building and demolition permits. The survey covers 2,600 municipalities, representing about 94 per cent of the population. The survey distinguishes residential, industrial, commercial, and institutional components and within the residential sector separates single- from multi-family dwellings. The latter is subject to significant monthly fluctuations because of large projects. The value of planned construction activities excludes engineering components (such as sewers and culverts) and land. Data appear for each province as well as for Canada as a whole.

Car Sales

Key numbers: domestic and imported cars and commercial vehicles (number of units sold, seasonally adjusted)
Reporting agency and source publication: StatsCan, *New Motor Vehicle Sales*, #63-007-XIB; StatsCan *Daily*
Website: www.statcan.ca
Usual timing: second week of the month (8:30 a.m.)
Reference period: second month before release
Revisions: usually minor; SA data revised one month after first release; NSA data revised once a year, along with SA data for latest four years, in December

Significance

Passenger cars include those used for personal and commercial purposes (such as taxis and rental cars). Trucks include minivans, sport utility vehicles, light and heavy trucks, vans, coaches, and buses.

Car sales are a valuable indicator of consumers' confidence and willingness to spend, since they can easily be brought forward or postponed. Month-to-month volatility is considerable, however, so it can be useful to chart new data against three or four years of monthly observations to get a feeling for the trend.

Consumer Price Index (CPI)

Key numbers: the All Items Consumer Price Index (SA) and its component indexes for Food, Shelter, Household Operations and Furnishings, Clothing and Footwear, Transportation, Health and Personal Care, Recreation, Education and Reading, and Alcoholic Beverages and Tobacco Products. The Energy component in the CPI, and the CPI excluding Food and Energy index, are also of interest. Indexes indicate percentage change from previous month and year earlier.

Reporting agency and source publications: StatsCan, *The Consumer Price Index*, #62-001-XPB; StatsCan *Daily*. See also the StatsCan's *Consumer Price Index Reference Paper*, #62-553. The website provides current data on release and has *Your Guide to the Consumer Price Index*, #62-557-XPB, available for downloading.

Website: www.statcan.ca

Usual timing: generally second or third week of month (seven a.m.); release dates published in advance on website

Reference period: previous month

Revisions: none

Description

The CPI measures the prices paid by Canadian consumers for a fixed basket of goods and services. StatsCan updates the goods and services in the CPI basket every four years or so. The goods and services in the basket, weighted to reflect the purchasing habits of families and individuals living in urban and rural private households, are priced every month in cities across the country. CPIs appear for Canada, for each province, and for the cities of Whitehorse and Yellowknife. (All-items and shelter cost indexes appear for major cities as well.) The price of each item is indexed to a base period, currently 1996. The resulting individual price indexes are then combined into a weighted average to produce the overall CPI. Table 14 gives the weights that correspond to the cost of the 1996 basket of consumer goods and services (based on the 1996 Family Expenditure Survey and the 1996 Family Food Expenditure Survey) when expressed in the prices of December 1997. Note that these weights do not represent actual consumer expenditures in December 1997 – they represent the hypothetical cost of the 1996 basket of commodities, had it been purchased at December 1997 prices.

TABLE 14
Weights in the Canadian CPI, 1996

	1996 basket at 1996 prices		1996 basket at December 1997 prices	
All items	100.0		100.0	
Food	17.84		17.89	
Food purchased from stores		12.88		12.91
Food purchased from restaurants		4.96		4.98
Shelter	27.12		26.75	
Rented accommodation		7.24		7.17
Owned accommodation		15.33		14.95
Water, fuel, and electricity		4.55		4.64
Household operations and furnishings	10.71		10.76	
Household operations		6.79		6.90
Household furnishings		3.93		3.86
Clothing and footwear	6.33		6.25	
Clothing		4.23		4.17
Footwear		0.94		0.93
Clothing, accessories, and jewellery		0.58		0.55
Clothing material, notions, and services		0.59		0.59
Transportation	18.59		18.96	
Private transportation		17.13		17.34
Public transportation		1.46		1.63
Health and personal care	4.61		4.60	
Health care		2.12		2.11
Personal care		2.50		2.49
Recreation, education, and reading	11.34		11.25	
Recreation		8.89		8.58
Education		1.72		1.92
Reading material and other printed matter		0.72		0.75
Alcoholic beverages and tobacco products	3.45		3.54	
Alcoholic beverages		1.86		1.87
Tobacco products and smokers' supplies		1.59		1.66

Source: Statistics Canada, The Consumer Price Index, #62-001-XPB (Feb. 1998).

Significance

The CPI is by far the most commonly cited measure of inflation, in part because of its reliability. It is never revised, since the complete pre-set survey is carried out every month. It is timely; it provides a detailed picture of consumer prices in each province and for Canada, just three weeks after the end of the reference month. However, it has some limitations. First, though Statscan substitutes different goods and services when necessary to maintain the intention of the basket, it ignores many of the substitutions that consumers make in response to price changes or changes in preferences. Since such substitutions often involve buying more of a less expensive good, the CPI may overestimate the actual increase in prices paid by consumers. Second, some components, such as the prices of fresh fruit and vegetables, are highly volatile. Third, the CPI refers only to consumer prices, whose trend may diverge from the direction of other prices in the economy, and in any case it does not cover all the elements in family expenditure (for example, income taxes or financial and legal services). A good article on biases in the CPI appeared in the *Bank of Canada Review* (spring 1998).

A broader measure of the prices paid by households is the implicit deflator for personal expenditure on goods and services published quarterly in the **NIEA**. Here, the weights are recalculated each quarter to reflect changes in spending patterns. Generally, however, the two measures track each other very closely.

Many analysts watch the so-called core rate of CPI inflation, which removes the volatile food and energy components from the index. It is not really a core rate, however, because transitory or special events can affect it. The Bank of Canada's inflation target is expressed in terms of the All-Items CPI, but the Bank pays close attention to a version of the CPI that omits food and energy prices and indirect taxes – the first two because of their volatility and the latter because they are set administratively and do not reflect trends in demand or supply.

Differences from U.S. CPI

The Canadian and U.S. indexes are similar in most respects. Nevertheless, two differences in weighting and coverage deserve special note. In the United States, where consumers bear much more of the cost of medical care, its CPI more heavily weights these costs. Also, the U.S. CPI measures homeowners' costs using a rental-equivalence approach, while Canada applies a user-cost method. (See U.S. **Consumer Price Index**).

Durable Goods Orders

Key numbers: total new orders for durable goods (percentage change from previous month and year earlier)
Reporting agency and source publication: StatsCan, *Monthly Survey of Manufacturing*, #31-001; StatsCan *Daily*; and see **Business Conditions Survey**

Website: www.statcan.ca
Usual timing: forty-five days after the end of the reference month
Reference period: second month before release
Revisions: three months; annual revision, usually in June, reflecting additional data collected by the annual Census of Manufacturers

Significance

New orders for durable goods (items produced by the following industries: wood, furniture and fixtures, primary metal, fabricated metal products, machinery, transportation equipment, electrical and electronic products, and non-metallic mineral products) serve widely as a leading indicator of strength or weakness in the economy, on the view that they reflect business confidence in the same way as car sales signal consumer confidence. Note, however, that orders can be shipped during the same month in which they were received, so the figures do not necessarily relate to future production levels. In addition, not all orders will be filled from Canadian factory shipments; some may be subcontracted to foreign suppliers. Month-to-month volatility in orders is considerable, so it is useful to chart the data in order to assess the developing trend.

Employment and Unemployment

Key numbers: change in employment; unemployment rate
Reporting agency and source publication: StatsCan, *Labour Force Information*, #71-001-PPB; StatsCan *Daily*. See also StatsCan's *The Labour Force*, #71-005-XPB, a quarterly publication featuring analytical articles. The method of the Labour Force Survey (LFS) is explained in *Guide to the Labour Force Survey*, downloadable from the website.
Website: www.statcan.ca
Usual timing: Friday of first full week of month (7:00 a.m.) following reference month
Reference period: week containing fifteenth of month
Survey period: week following reference week
Revisions: survey data not revised monthly; seasonal factors for three years back revised annually with January release; benchmark revisions based on new census data carried out every five years

Description

The 'labour force' refers to those members of the civilian non-institutional population fifteen years of age or over who are available for work during a reference week. For LFS purposes, work is any work for pay or profit, whether an employer–employee relationship or self-employment. It also includes unpaid family work that contributes directly to the operation of a farm, business, or professional practice owned or operated by a related member of the household, but not unpaid domestic work. It regards persons as available if they could have worked if a suitable job had been offered or if the reason that they could not take a job was of a temporary nature, such as illness or disability, personal or family responsibilities, a job starting soon, or vacation. Employed persons are those who during the reference week did any work at all at a job or business or had a job but were not at work because of illness, strike, vacation, or certain other contingencies. The unemployed represent the rest of the labour force. They had no work and had actively looked for work during the past four weeks, had been on temporary layoff with an expectation of recall, or had a new job starting in no more than four weeks.

The LFS surveys about 52,000 households by personal interview or by telephone (dwellings remain in the survey sample for six months, with one-sixth of the sample being replaced each month). LFS obtains information for all civilian household members fifteen years of age or older. It classifies data by age group, sex, educational attainment, union status, and family status of the respondent, and by occupation, by industry, by size of firm, and by province. (Yukon and the Northwest Territories are excluded.) The survey also captures data on wages and salaries, regular and overtime hours worked per week, full- or part-time status, and reasons for job termination. (Full-time employed consist of persons who usually work thirty hours or more per week at their main or only job.)

Significance

The unemployment rate is an important indicator of tightness in the market for labour, a critical input in every production process. Generally speaking, the lower the rate, the more the balance leans towards a sellers' market for labour services, and the likelier it is that wage increases will pick up.

Reliability and Limitations

While the unemployment rate is a handy indicator of labour-market tightness, its interpretation is complicated by fluctuations in the number of individuals who decide to participate in the labour force. The participation rate, especially of younger workers, is very sensitive to employment opportunities. This can sometimes result in anomalies such as a rising unemployment rate in a month when employment is growing. It is therefore desirable to follow other indicators available from the survey, such as changes in the level of employment, the proportion of each age and sex group actually participating in the labour force, and the ratio of employment to the population of working-force age.

The geographical and industrial breakdown of employment growth provides a sensitive indication of areas of strength and weakness in the economy, and the ratio of full- to part-time employment serves widely as an indicator of 'job quality' and, indirectly, consumer confidence.

Major Differences with U.S. Unemployment Rate

The concept of the unemployment rate is similar in Canada and the United States, but differences in the treatment of certain items can make comparisons inappropriate:

- The relevant age group in the United States is sixteen and over (in Canada, fifteen and over).
- Canadian unemployed include those using any job-search methods; the U.S. definition of active job search excludes, for instance, reading the newspaper.
- In Canada, persons not working by reason of layoff are counted as unemployed if they have a definite date or an indication from their employer of recall; in the United States, they are dropped from the labour force after thirty days.

These differences in measurement bias the Canadian rate upward relative to the U.S. rate.

Federal Government Fiscal Position

Key numbers: budgetary surplus or deficit; financial requirements excluding foreign-exchange transactions

Reporting agency and source publication: Finance Canada, monthly *Fiscal Monitor*. Finance Canada publishes a number of documents each year, including the annual budget, giving the government's view of its fiscal position and its strategy for dealing with its debt. These can generally be obtained on the website or ordered through it.

Website: www.fin.gc.ca

Usual timing: second or third week of month

Reference period: second month before release

Revisions: none, but data in *Fiscal Monitor* preliminary; revisions incorporated in Public Accounts when tabled, usually many months after the end of the fiscal year in March

Description

The *Fiscal Monitor* contains a monthly and fiscal-year-to-date account of federal revenues, expenditures, and financial transactions, presented on a budgetary basis. Federal, provincial, and local government revenues and expenditures appear quarterly in the **NIEA** on a National Accounts basis. The quarterly *Bank of Canada Review*, Table G-1, provides some of the data on both bases of accounting. *Fiscal Reference Tables*, published annually in October by Finance Canada, provides annual data on the financial position of federal and individual provincial governments on a budgetary basis. See chapter 9 for a brief explanation of the differences between the two bases of accounting.

Help-Wanted Index

Key numbers: index-level (SAAR) and percentage change from previous month
Reporting agency and source publication: StatsCan *Daily*
Website: www.statcan.ca
Usual timing: Wednesday of first or second week of the month (10:00 a.m.)
Reference period: previous month
Revisions: three months; annual revision in March for four years of history

Description

Canada's Help-Wanted Index is patterned after the U.S. **Help-Wanted Index** developed by the U.S. Conference Board. It surveys newspapers in twenty Canadian metropolitan areas. The base year for the index is 1991. Whereas the U.S. Conference Board uses a monthly survey, which requests total want-ad volume for the month, which it then adjusts for the length of the month and the number of Sundays (ad volume usually increases on Sundays), the Canadian survey takes place on the Saturday of the week containing the fifteenth of the month, which may make it less representative of monthly want-ad volume. In addition, Statistics Canada compiles the regional and national indexes by weighting the city indexes by their respective populations; the U.S. survey, by non-agricultural employment in each city. If data for a particular newspaper are missing on the survey date, StatsCan will use the previous Saturday if available. If this is not available, it uses results for other newspapers in the region to estimate those of the missing paper.

Significance

The Help-Wanted Index is the only indicator that reports on the 'demand side' of Canadian urban labour markets.

Housing Starts

Key numbers: total housing starts, all areas (SAAR)
Reporting agency and source publication: Canada Mortgage and Housing Corporation (CMHC). CMHC's *Housing Information Monthly*, published with a lag of one or two months, provides very detailed tables on starts, completions, units under construction, and more. CMHC also publishes an annual compendium, *Canadian Housing Statistics*, in May, accompanied by a brief monthly supplement, *Monthly Housing Statistics*.
Websites: www.cmhc-schl.gc.ca and www.chmos-sd-mloc.ceds.com
Usual timing: preliminary on sixth day of month (8:15 a.m.), revised with release for following month
Reference period: previous month
Revisions: one month; also, a fuller revision once a quarter; annual revision, usually in January, for two years of history (SAAR figures only)

Description

A housing start is a dwelling unit on which construction has begun during the month. A start is usually associated with the pouring of concrete for the foundation. In the case of a multiple-unit structure, such as an apartment building, the total number of units is credited to the month in which the foundation is poured.

CMHC bases the urban component of its monthly housing-start figures on enumeration; it bases the estimate of rural starts on historical ratios between urban and rural housing activity. It releases quarterly estimates at the end of the month following the reference quarter. Unlike the monthly figures, the quarterly estimate is based on a survey of rural housing starts as well as on the enumeration of starts in urban areas with a population of 10,000 or more.

Significance

Residential construction is a relatively small, but highly volatile component of the economy, accounting on average for about 7 per cent of real GDE. Construction of new dwellings accounts for about half of it and can be tracked quite effectively by monitoring housing starts. But renovation, which is not captured in the data on starts, has become a growing component of residential construction activity. Real estate commissions and other ownership transfer costs comprise the remaining one-sixth of residential construction expenditures and of course relate to the sale of existing homes as well as new ones.

Index of Leading Indicators

Key numbers: composite Leading Indicator (smoothed), percentage change from previous month
Reporting agency and source publication: StatsCan, *Canadian Economic Observer*, #11-010-XPB; StatsCan *Daily*
Website: www.statcan.ca
Usual timing: two to three weeks after reference month
Reference period: month before release
Revisions: five months back

Description

The ten components of the Composite Index of Leading Indicators are: Retail Sales, Furniture and Appliances; Retail Sales, other Durable Goods; Housing Index; United States Composite Leading Index; Shipment to Inventory ratio for Finished Goods in Manufacturing Industries; New Orders for Durable Goods; Average Workweek in Manufacturing; Employment in Business and Personal Services; TSE 300 Stock Price Index; Money Supply (M1).

Significance

The Canadian Index of Leading Indicators and the U.S. **Index of Leading Indicators** are very similar in construction, designed to anticipate emerging trends in economic activity. In Canada, where services now account for approximately 60 per cent of production and 70 per cent of employment, an indicator of strength in services is now included in the Leading Index; the U.S. Leading Index has no services component. The Canadian Index includes the U.S. Leading Index; Canadian exports account for close to 40 per cent of real GDP, and about 80 per cent of them go to the United States, so an upswing or downturn in U.S. economic activity will have major repercussions on Canada's output, indicated by inclusion of the U.S. Leading Index.

Reliability and Limitations

Chart 26 compares the percentage change of the unsmoothed index with that of real GDP from one quarter to the next between 1980 and 1997. False signals do not seem to be a particular problem, but the index does not appear to provide a reliably long lead either, on this comparison. The longest-leading component of the index at peaks is M1, followed by the TSE 300, housing starts, and average workweek. If these three should all begin to decline, the implication of a coming economic slowdown is very strong. (Chart 15 illustrates the strong lead characteristic of M1.)

Revisions to the Canadian Leading Index are smaller than those made to the U.S. Index – On average, the Canadian index changes about 0.2 per cent from preliminary release.

Industrial Product Price Index (IPPI)

Key numbers: IPPI Total All commodities (NSA), percentage change from previous month
Reporting agency and source publication: StatsCan, *Industry Price Indexes*, #62-011-XPB; Statscan *Daily*
Website: www.statcan.ca
Usual timing: about four weeks after end of reference month (8:30 a.m.), at the same time as **Raw Materials Price Index**; release dates published a year in advance
Reference period: previous month
Survey period: fifteenth of the month or nearest prior business day
Revisions: previous six months

Description

The IPPI is a composite of price indexes (1992 = 100) designed to measure the prices of manufactured goods as they leave the factory gate. Since the goods are valued at the boundary of the establishment, the IPPI excludes the effect of sales taxes, excise taxes, transportation costs, and distributors' margins.

The IPPI monitors prices in about one-quarter of the economy. It covers commodities produced by domestic manufacturers, wholly or partly with Canadian labour and materials, and it includes sales to other Canadian businesses, individuals, governments, and foreign markets. Canadian exporters often quote prices in foreign currencies, especially for motor vehicles, pulp and paper, and

Chart 26. Change in Leading Indicators versus change in real GDP, 1980–97

Quarterly % change   Quarterly % change

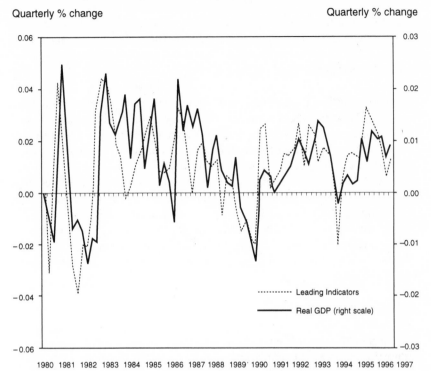

Sources: Statistics Canada, CANSIM database, series D14872 (seasonally adjusted real
GDP, percentage change from previous quarter) and D100030 (unsmoothed *Index of
Leading Indicators*, percentage change of quarterly average).

wood products. This makes the IPPI sensitive to the exchange rate – it is
estimated that a 1 per cent change in the value of the Canadian dollar against
the U.S. dollar may change the IPPI by approximately 0.2 per cent. The IPPI
does not cover manufactured goods that are imported and resold by Canadian
manufacturers.

Aggregate IPPI is a fixed-weight index. The weights assigned to the individual commodities are based on the 1992 output matrix of the input/output
(I/O) system. (The matrix shows what proportion of each industry's inputs
derive from each industry's output.) About 10,000 prices are collected monthly
from about 3,500 producers.

Significance

The IPPI measures the prices at which new manufacturing orders are transacted, thereby capturing cost pressures that may later affect the consumer level.

Reliability and Limitations

Though the IPPI is a useful harbinger of consumer price movements, it has a number of limitations as a predictor of consumer-level inflation. Since it covers only manufactured goods, it does not capture price movements in service sectors of the economy, which account for half of consumer spending in Canada. Nor does it capture changes in wholesale or retail markups.

Like all fixed-weight indexes, the IPPI tends to overestimate cost pressures, especially in times of rapid inflation and rapid rates of introduction of new commodities, since it does not, except when rebased, account for changing buying patterns of purchasers. The substitution of more expensive commodities by cheaper ones goes on continually, but the motivation to do so will be greater when particular commodities' prices rise or fall sharply for reasons specific to them.

Industrial Production

Key numbers: industrial production, percentage change from previous month
Reporting agency and source publication: StatsCan, *Gross Domestic Product by Industry*, #15-001-XPB; StatsCan *Daily*
Website: www.statcan.ca
Usual timing: final business day of the month, with **Real GDP at Factor Cost** (10:00 a.m.)
Reference period: second month before release
Revisions: previous four months; annual revision in June for five years of history

Description

Statistics Canada publishes estimates of industrial production monthly as part of its release of data on Real GDP at Factor Cost. 'Industrial production' – the output of the manufacturing, mining, and utilities sectors – accounted for 75 per cent of goods produced in 1997 but only 25 per cent of Real GDP at Factor Cost.

In an economy increasingly dominated by services, industrial production is no longer as important as it once was. But the swings in industrial production are greater typically than those in the output of service industries, so the economy's overall variability is still dominated by this area. Canada's exports too are dominated by industrial output rather than by services. Its sensitivity to international fluctuations is therefore largely transmitted through the industrial sectors (though its sensitivity to international financial-market conditions is also very important). As a leading indicator, however, industrial production is not helpful, because its cycles tend to coincide with those of the economy as a whole.

Merchandise Trade

Key numbers: merchandise exports and imports, the trade balance, and price and volume indexes (SA, BOP basis)
Reporting agency and source publication: StatsCan, *Canadian International Merchandise Trade*, #65-001-XPB; StatsCan *Daily*
Website: www.statcan.ca
Usual timing: mid-month (7:00 a.m.)
Reference period: second month before release
Survey period: entire month
Revisions: year-to-date, often large; annual revision in June for data from previous four years

Description

The source for most of the import data is the documentation provided to Revenue Canada by importers. It is a census of all transactions. Estimates of Canada's exports to the United States are based on import data collected by U.S. Customs and compiled by the U.S. Bureau of the Census. In a similar manner, the United States now bases its estimates of U.S. exports to Canada on the import data collected by Revenue Canada and compiled by Statistics Canada. Prior to 1990, each country collected its own export estimates, but their reliability was relatively weak; import documents are on the whole more rigorously controlled than export documents. StatsCan reconciles its trade data with other countries on a less frequent basis.

The data include all goods that have crossed Canadian borders, except – in order to conform with UN-developed trade concepts and methods – exports and imports by Canadian and foreign diplomatic or military delegations or personnel; purchases or sales of supplies for ships or aircraft engaged in international traffic; settlers' effects; goods intended to be returned to the exporting country within a short period, such as works of art loaned for exhibition, vehicles exported for racing, and items exported for repairs; and financial assets such as coins, monetary gold, stocks, and bonds.

The data appear in two versions: the Customs basis and the Balance of Payments (BOP) basis. The latter version, which conforms to SNA concepts and definitions, derives from the former by adjustments related to trade definition, valuation, and timing. The principal difference between the two is that Customs-based statistics cover the physical movement of goods as reflected on customs documents, while BOP-adjusted data are intended to cover all economic transactions between residents and non-residents that involve merchandise trade. On the Customs basis, imported goods are valued FOB ('free on board') at the original shipment point, excluding freight and insurance to the Canadian port of entry, while imports on the BOP basis include the value of inland freight to the border of the exporting country. In both systems, exports are valued FOB the port of exit from Canada, including domestic freight charges to that point. See **Balance of Payments**.

Domestic exports include goods of foreign origin that have been materially transformed in Canada; 're-exports' have not been materially transformed here (for example, foreign-made parts included in goods assembled in Canada).

Significance

Statistics Canada uses the merchandise trade figures as direct inputs into its estimates of GDE. Since the monthly series divides the export and import values into volume and price components, it is easy in principle to anticipate the quarterly GDE estimates: they are simply the sum of the monthly values, with averages of the monthly export and import price deflators used to derive volumes. In practice, however, the data are subject to substantial revisions from month to month and between the last monthly release of a given quarter and the release of that quarter's GDE, so use them with caution.

Reliability and Limitations

The fact that the data on merchandise exports and imports are presented on a National Accounts (BOP) basis is convenient for forecasters because of the ready way in which they can be used in tracking the relevant quarter's GDE and because the division between volumes and prices facilitates analysis of the influences on the Canadian trade balance. However, the complexity of the exercise, the possibility of substantial under-reporting, and the lags involved with some of the data (flows of electricity and piped oil and natural gas are reported with a one-month lag; the latest month's figures are estimates) make the series less than reliable. Note too that some exports reported as going to the United States are intended for trans-shipment to third countries, but exporters may avoid reporting them as such in order to avoid time-consuming administrative procedures. The extent to which this phenomenon results in an over-statement of Canadian exports to the United States relative to total Canadian exports is not known.

Monetary Conditions Index (MCI)

Key numbers: MCI
Reporting agency and source publication: Bank of Canada, *Weekly Financial Statistics*
Website: www.bank-banque-canada.ca
Usual timing: Friday after 2.00 p.m.
Reference period: current week
Revisions: none

See Chart 17 above. The Bank of Canada publishes this index to provide the public with a convenient way of assessing the stance of monetary policy. As was discussed in chapters 5 and 7, in order to control inflation the Bank must influence the level of aggregate demand. Its ability to control the overnight interest rate provides it with leverage over the entire structure of nominal and real interest rates. This control in turn, when market participants assess it against the competing attractions of interest rates abroad, motivates short-term capital flows into and out of Canada and thus puts upward or downward pressure on nominal and real exchange rates. Since investment in capital goods is sensitive to real interest rates, exports and imports are sensitive to real exchange rates, and aggregate demand as a whole responds to shifts in these components through the multiplier process, the Bank can, with patience and persistence, achieve its ends. The Bank's task is eased if market participants understand its intentions (as long as they expect it to be successful; if not, they may not follow its lead). The MCI is based on a weighted average of nominal short-term interest rates and nominal exchange rates; a persistent rise or fall over a month or more signals a shift towards restraint or stimulus, respectively.

Technically, the Bank of Canada constructs the MCI in three steps:

- First, it takes the current level of the ninety-day commercial paper rate (for example, 3.50 per cent) and multiplies it by three.
- Second, it adds the result to the current value of a weighted average of exchange rates for the Canadian dollar against its ten most important trading partners' currencies, weighted by trade.
- Third, it indexes this result (January 1987 = 0).

The interest rate receives three times as much weight as the exchange rate because the Bank's economic models suggest that the former has roughly three times as much influence on GDE. In principle the MCI should reflect real, not nominal interest and exchange rates, but that would make it more difficult for the public to grasp and would reduce its usefulness as a communications device.

Money and Credit Aggregates

Key numbers: M1, M2, M2+, household credit, residential mortgage credit, short-term business credit
Reporting agency and source publications: Bank of Canada, *Weekly Financial Statistics*, and quarterly *Bank of Canada Review* (*BCR*), Tables E1 and E2
Website: www.bank-banque-canada.ca
Usual timing: monthly data on monetary aggregates available on second Friday of following month (after 2:00 p.m.)
Reference period: previous month, except data on household credit, which are not available until two months after reference month
Survey period: monthly average
Revisions: frequent, mostly to recent months, but occasionally back further

Description

See Tables 8 and 9 above. The Bank of Canada presents monetary and credit data on both an SA and NSA basis. The **Financial Flow Accounts**, the **National Balance Sheet Accounts**, and the **National Income and Expenditure Accounts** publish each sector's transactions in financial assets and liabilities each quarter, integrated with changes in sectoral balance sheets, also SA and NSA. Generally the data from both sources show the same trends over time, but the FFA mortgage data refer to all mortgages held by persons and unincorporated businesses, making no differentiation between residential and non-residential mortgages. The Bank of Canada's data do distinguish the two. Both the FFA and the *BCR* indicate the intermediaries involved in consumer-credit and residential-mortgage lending, such as the chartered banks and the trust companies. The *BCR* (Table C7) also provides a breakdown of quarterly bank lending by detailed categories: auto loans, loans for mobile homes, loans to purchase or carry securities, and credit-card loans.

Significance

When consumers increase their debt, they use it to increase their assets at the same time. Consumer borrowing is strongly related to the demand for consumer durables, such as autos, and for home ownership, which in turn is affected by the age structure of the working population, the average age of cars on the road, attitudes towards accommodation-sharing, family size, and so on. But the decision to undertake debt is not related simply to purchases of big, lumpy assets. Consumers' 'comfort level' with debt, relative to their net worth, reflects the state of their confidence not only in the future value of the assets being financed but, even more, in their expectations of their ability to service the debt from future income. Employment and labour-compensation trends are thus major determinants of credit use.

From time to time, consumers' and businesses' debt-carrying capacity (as assessed both by themselves and by potential lenders) may be significantly underused, which helps to explain why, even when market interest rates are rising sharply, borrowers may continue to expand their reliance on credit rapidly for some time.

Raw Materials Price Index (RMPI)

Key numbers: RMPI (NSA), percentage change from previous month
Reporting agency and source publication: StatsCan, *Industry Price Indexes*, #62-011-XPB; StatsCan *Daily*
Website: www.statcan.ca
Usual timing: about four weeks after end of reference month, released with **IPPI** (8:30 a.m.)
Reference period: previous month
Survey period: fifteenth of month or nearest prior business day
Revisions: previous six months

Description

The RMPI measures the prices paid by Canadian industries to purchase raw materials, which are either a commodity that is sold for the first time after being extracted from nature or a substitutable recycled product (such as scrap metal). The index prices approximately eighty commodities, grouped into seven major categories. Their index weights come from the 1992 Input–Output Table, from StatsCan's Input–Output Division.

The index covers domestically produced and imported goods purchased by Canadian industries, generally for further processing. It does not cover exported commodities as such, nor does it examine the prices of raw materials such as foods that flow directly to consumers. Since the RMPI is a purchasers' price index, it includes transportation charges, taxes, and customs duties, as well as the effects of price subsidies.

Significance and Limitations

The RMPI's uses parallel those of the IPPI. It is often read as a leading indicator of inflation. However, it is not as helpful a predictor of the direction of general price trends as the IPPI. Some raw materials can be processed and ready for consumption within days, while others require much longer and influence retail prices only with a significant lag. The RMPI also suffers from the limitations associated with fixed-weight price indexes. When a commodity's price jumps, its users can often substitute others for it fairly rapidly, so that their costs do not rise as much as the index suggests. Also, though prices of raw materials tend to be relatively volatile, they are typically only a small component of overall business costs. Raw materials contribute far less than labour to the overall costs of industrial production.

Real GDP at Factor Cost

Key numbers: GDP at Factor Cost at 1992 prices (SAAR), percentage change from previous month
Reporting agency and source publications: StatsCan, *Gross Domestic Product by Industry*, #15-001-XPB; StatsCan *Daily*
Website: www.statcan.ca
Usual timing: final business day of month at same time as Index of **Industrial Production** (10:00 a.m.)
Reference period: second month before release
Revisions: annual revisions in June (released at end of August), affecting five years of history and incorporating new annual benchmark information compiled by StatsCan's Input–Output Division; between annual revisions, monthly estimates revised back to January of most recent year in which annual revision was made, reflecting both new data and new seasonal factors

Description

Every month StatsCan releases estimates of economic production within Canada's borders. These estimates differ in two major respects from the quarterly GDE estimates in the **National Income and Expenditure Accounts (NIEA)**. First, they show output on an industry-by-industry basis, while the quarterly data are aggregated by type of final demand expenditure, such as personal consumption, government spending, and business investment. Second, the monthly numbers are estimated at factor cost only, whereas the quarterly estimates are calculated both at market prices and at factor cost. Market prices include the effect of indirect taxes and subsidies as well as factor costs. Since indirect taxes fall more heavily on some products than on others, the contribution of specific industries to production is better measured if they are not included.

The two types of estimate are derived partly from different data or, when using the same data, may place different weights on the various sources. Therefore, while tracking the monthly GDP is helpful in forecasting the quarterly GDP, the relationship between the two is not one to one. Thus the three monthly numbers do not necessarily add up to the quarterly NIEA figure. But the monthly and quarterly data rarely give a substantially different view of the pace of economic growth.

In total, the monthly GDP estimates cover 310 industries, industry aggregations, and groupings, based on the 1980 Standard Industrial Classification. Aggregations appear for business and non-business output and for goods and service industries within those categories. GDP for a single industry is referred to as 'value added' in that industry. Output is divided into eighteen broad categories, as shown in Table 15. The output of the manufacturing and mining industries and 'other utilities' is included in the Index of **Industrial Production**.

Retail Trade

Key numbers: total retail sales (SA), retail sales excluding autos (SA), percentage change from previous month

Reporting agency and source publication: StatsCan, #63-005-XPB; StatsCan *Daily*

Website: www.statcan.ca

Usual timing: 20th to 25th of month, 8:30 a.m.

Reference period: second month before release

Revisions: each month, three months back for SA, one month for NSA data; annual revision in April for four years of SA, one year of NSA data

TABLE 15
Real GDP at Factor Cost, 1997

Division	$million (1997)	% of GDP at factor cost
Agricultural and related services	12,264	1.8
Fishing and trapping	893	0.1
Logging and forestry	4,132	0.6
Mining, quarrying, and oil wells	28,175	4.1
Manufacturing	121,999	17.6
Construction	39,062	5.6
Transportation and storage services	29,645	4.3
Communication and other utilities	49,703	7.2
Wholesale trade	40,135	5.8
Retail trade	40,618	5.9
Finance and insurance	36,027	5.2
Real estate operators and insurance agents	74,431	10.8
Business services	38,837	5.6
Government services	40,558	5.9
Educational services	40,221	5.8
Health and social services	48,516	7.0
Accommodation, food and beverage services	18,394	2.7
Other service industries	28,015	4.1
Total	691,625	100.0

Source: Statistics Canada, Gross Domestic Product by Industry, #15-001-XPB.

Description

Statistics Canada releases retail trade estimates on a monthly basis for each province, territory, and major metropolitan area and also for each of sixteen store types (such as shoe stores and gasoline service stations). The estimates do not include any form of direct selling (for example, vending machines, door to door, record club sales). They exclude sales taxes and adjust the sales figures for returns and discounts. Statistics Canada bases the release on monthly mail and telephone surveys; each month it samples all the large enterprises (such as department stores and chains) but only a representative panel of smaller, single-establishment firms.

Statistics Canada estimates the retail trade data in terms of both current and constant dollars. It releases both seasonally adjusted and non-adjusted data, but because of the pronounced seasonal patterns in retail sales, unadjusted data do not provide a very useful guide to the underlying momentum of consumer spending.

Significance

Retail sales are unquestionably the best single monthly indicator of consumer spending. The retail sector handles the sale of most goods to the consumer, and goods account for almost half of total personal consumption. But the sale of services is largely excluded.

A changing trend in total retail sales normally indicates a pickup or slow-down in the economy's growth rate as a whole. Purchases of new motor vehicles in particular are strongly cyclical, since these are momentous, post-ponable decisions for the family and thus reflect the state of overall consumer confidence. Sales of furniture and household goods, strongly correlated with housing starts, also tend to be cyclical. However, while weakening growth in retail sales generally implies a slowdown in the economy, imported goods, which account for a very large share of sales, tend to share more than propor-tionally in the cycles of strength and weakness. On the one hand, they are heavily represented in the durable goods categories, whose demand fluctuates sharply with the cycle, and on the other hand, they may be marginal contribu-tors to sales where demand is less volatile. Thus imports often absorb more than their share of the impact of changes in the pace of consumer spending, reducing the cyclical nature of domestic production and overall GDP.

Reliability

Overall, data on retail sales are generally reliable at the trade-group level, but estimates are frequently revised to include reports received late from individual retailers.

Wage Settlements

Key number: average effective increase in base rates, in percentages
Reporting agency and source publication: Labour Canada, Bureau of Labour Information (BLI), *The Wage Settlements Bulletin*; StatsCan *Daily*
Website: www.statcan.ca
Usual timing: one to two months after previous quarter
Reference period: previous quarter
Revisions: several quarters

Description

Labour Canada releases monthly, quarterly, and annual averages of increases negotiated in wage settlements covering 500 or more employees. They cover all industries and jurisdictions across Canada. In early 1991 the BLI survey covered 1,094 agreements for 2.2 million employees – approximately 55 per cent of the unionized workforce and 20 per cent of non-farm paid employment.

For purposes of the survey, 'wage increases' refers to changes in base wage rates. Typically a collective bargaining agreement covers a wide spectrum of job classifications, each with its own wage structure. The base rate used in the calculations is the wage rate of the lowest-paid classification containing a significant number of qualified workers in the bargaining unit. The increase in the base rate does not necessarily reflect the average increase of all wages in the unit. Depending on the agreement, changes in the base rate can either overstate or underestimate the actual change in average wage rates covered by that agreement. Settlements can be arrived at for one, two, or three years, or for other periods. Often they are at least partly retroactive, having been delayed for one reason or another.

Many wage settlements currently carry cost-of-living-adjustment (COLA) clauses that partially (or, rarely, fully) index wage increases to changes in the CPI. Labour Canada reports effective wage increases for agreements with COLA clauses, based on actual and forecast CPI inflation.

The BLI reports changes in base wage rates by region for all industries, for private-sector industries, and for the public sector. It reports changes in all one-year, all two-year, and all three-year settlements separately, as well as the total. The five regions are the Atlantic provinces, Quebec, Ontario, the Prairie provinces, and British Columbia.

Wage settlements are a problematic indicator of inflation. The number of contracts settled in a given month or quarter can vary markedly. In quarters with a light collective-bargaining calendar, a particular agreement can often skew the aggregate numbers in a highly misleading manner. Nor does the BLI capture non-wage forms of labour compensation, such as pension-plan enrichments and other benefits.

Revisions are normally relatively minor. Settlements originally surveyed by phone are sometimes revised when printed copies of the agreements become available. Also, as new CPI information becomes available, the effective rate in agreements with COLA clauses must be recomputed. Of course, inflation forecasts change as well, requiring further adjustments to Labour Canada's projection of effective increases in COLA-based settlements.

QUARTERLY INDICATORS

Balance of Payments

Key number: current account balance
Reporting agency and source publications: StatsCan, *Canada's Balance of International Payments*, #67-001-XPB; StatsCan *Daily*; StatsCan, *Security Transactions with Non-Residents*, #67-202-XPB, and *The Canadian Balance of International Payments and International Investment Position: A Description of Sources and Methods*, #67-506E.
Website: www.statcan.ca
Usual timing: with release of *NIEA*
Reference period: previous quarter
Survey period: entire quarter
Revisions: year to date; four or five years with the first quarter data

Description

#67-001-XPB provides details on the bilateral accounts between Canada and the United States, the United Kingdom, other EU countries, Japan, other OECD countries, and all other countries, as well as the total for all countries. Special tables give details of investment income and receipts, transfers, and portfolio transactions in foreign and domestic securities by type and geographical area and of direct investment by industry and geographical area. **Merchandise Trade** data are adjusted from the basis on which they are reported to Customs to ensure consistency with Balance of Payments concepts and the SNA framework.

The data are presented both SA and NSA for the current account, but only on an NSA basis for the capital and financial accounts. See chapter 6 for a discussion of concepts.

Business Conditions Survey

Key number: percentage of responding firms expecting higher or lower production in next three months
Reporting agency and source publications: StatsCan **Daily**
Website: www.statcan.ca
Usual timing: first day of month (8.30 a.m.) following reference month
Reference period: January, April, July, and October

Survey period: majority of responses recorded in first two weeks of month; results based on replies from about 5,000 manufacturers and weighted by shipments or employment; except for data on production difficulties, data seasonally adjusted
Revisions: None

Description

This survey of manufacturers provides some insight into their expectations for production, employment, orders, and levels of finished-product inventory and their assessment of sources of difficulties in maintaining production (such as shortages of working capital or skilled labour).

Canada's International Investment Position

Key numbers: Canadian assets and liabilities abroad and non-residents' assets and liabilities in Canada (all data refer to year's end)
Reporting agency and source publication: StatsCan, *Canada's International Investment Position*, #67-202-XPB; StatsCan *Daily*; for helpful background: StatsCan, *The Canadian Balance of International Payments and International Investment Position: A Description of Sources and Methods*, #67-506E.
Website: www.statcan.ca
Usual timing: mid-year publication with preliminary data for two previous year's end and final data, with extended detail for earlier year's end
Survey period: annual

Description

Canada's International Investment Position is the balance sheet that presents the country's assets and liabilities with the rest of the world. It provides extensive detail on Canadian investment abroad and non-resident investment in Canada by type of asset and liability and by country. The position reflects not only financial transactions with non-residents but also valuation changes resulting from fluctuations in exchange rates, write-offs and revaluations of assets, the effects of migrations and inheritances, dilution of equity resulting from new issues of shares, and so on. The position records external assets and liabilities at the book values recorded in the balance sheets of the issuers of liabilities and equities. The calculation of Canada's net international investment position is reconciled with the quarterly **National Balance Sheet Accounts (NBSA)**.

Capacity Utilization Rate

Key number: capacity use (total of all industries)
Reporting agency and source publication: StatsCan, *Capacity Utilization Rates in Canadian Manufacturing*, #31-003; StatsCan *Daily*
Website: www.statcan.ca
Usual timing: third month after quarter's end
Reference period: previous quarter
Revisions: every quarter, three or four years revised
Description

StatsCan publishes a quarterly measure of capacity use for the manufacturing sector as a whole and for twenty-two industries, broadly grouped into durable and non-durable.

Significance

Capacity utilization is a measure of actual output divided by 'potential' output – the maximum production that would occur with full use of all plant and equipment as well as labour. Economists look to capacity use as an indicator of demand pressure as well as of investment spending. When the economy reaches full or near-full capacity, increases in demand generally lead quickly to a more rapid rate of inflation, since the economy has only limited ability to respond with greater supply, unless imports can satiate excess demand. Alternatively, if large amounts of excess capacity exist, an increase in demand is more likely to result in higher production volumes in faster price inflation.

Capital spending is also closely correlated with changes in capacity use over the business cycle. Typically, use of capacity remains low during the early phase of an economic expansion, discouraging investment. As the expansion matures, the economy approaches full capacity, triggering capital spending on new plant and equipment. Historically, late-cycle investment booms have often accompanied rising inflation, prompting central banks to tighten monetary conditions and slow the economy just as the additional capacity was entering service.

Limitations

Historical comparisons of utilization rates are suspect because of the many difficulties involved in measuring changes in the stock of capital over long periods.

Corporate Profits in the NIEA

This is one of three widely used sources of information published each quarter on aggregate Canadian corporate earnings, along with **Earnings on the TSE 300 Index** and StatsCan's **Quarterly Financial Statistics for Enterprises**.

Key numbers: Pre-tax profits; federal and provincial taxes on corporate income; after-tax profits; dividends and retained earnings
Reporting agency and source publication: StatsCan, *National Income and Expenditure Accounts*, #13-001-PPB, Tables 29 and 55
Usual timing: forty to sixty-five days after end of quarter
Reference period: previous quarter
Survey period: entire quarter (but treating a company's report of its profits for a period ending in first or second month of a quarter as that quarter's earnings, even though part from previous quarter)
Revisions: year to date, except for first quarter release, when revisions extend four years back

Description

The **National Income and Expenditure Accounts (NIEA)** provides estimates of pre-tax corporate profits on a domestic basis and a national basis, following the distinction between GDP and GNP. In principle, pre-tax profits on a domestic basis should include earnings in Canada attributable to foreign shareholders' capital, but not the earnings of Canadian-owned corporations from their foreign operations. Pre-tax profits on a national basis should include the corporate-source earnings of Canadian residents and exclude those of non-residents, regardless of the geographical location of the activity. In practice, pre-tax profits measured on a domestic basis exceed those on a national basis by the excess of interest and miscellaneous investment income paid to non-residents over interest, dividends, and miscellaneous investment income received from them. The *NIEA* subtracts taxes, dividends, and bad debts from pre-tax profits on a national basis to arrive at 'Undistributed Corporate Profits' – that is, retained earnings.

The SNA adjusts profits reported by companies to a base profit concept by excluding items such as capital gains and losses. (Concepts of income in the *NIEA* always refer to income from current production.) The relevant *NIEA* tables report corporate income taxes paid to federal and provincial governments. Dividends to Canadian residents appear separately from dividends to non-residents. Data on quarterly profits tend to be volatile, and revisions to pre-tax profits, tax liabilities, and dividends can be substantial.

StatsCan also publishes income statements and other financial data on an industry-by-industry basis in **Quarterly Financial Statistics for Enterprises.**

Earnings on the TSE 300 Index

Key Numbers: adjusted earnings
Reporting agency and source publication: TSE *Daily Record*; TSE *Review*
Usual timing: continuous
Reference period: past twelve months
Survey period: continuous
Revisions: none

Description

The Toronto Stock Exchange (TSE) calculates quarterly earnings for the 300 Composite Index as follows: total market earnings are the sum of earnings per share multiplied by the market float (shares available for trading) for each company. The calculation uses the latest quarterly earnings results; the earnings refer to profits after taxes and before extraordinary items. It then divides total market earnings into total market capitalization of the companies included in the TSE 300 to arrive at an aggregate ratio of price to earnings. It then divides the market index level by the aggregate price-to-earnings ratio to arrive at total earnings for the TSE 300 Index.

TSE 300 earnings are not seasonally adjusted. They generally summarize the profit performance of the larger listed Canadian companies.

The NIEA measure closest to TSE 300 earnings is after-tax profits. Significant differences in their annual growth rates often arise, however, as a result of the NIEA's more comprehensive coverage of firms large and small, public and private, and because of SNA conventions such as use of the base- profit concept (see above).

The closest measure to the TSE 300 earnings in the **Quarterly Financial Statistics for Enterprises** is After-tax Profits before Extraordinary Gains. Again, however, there are often significant differences in annual growth rates, largely because of differences in the weights assigned to industries by the two samples.

Financial Flow Accounts

See **National Economic and Financial Accounts,** part I, below.

National Balance Sheet Accounts (NBSA)

Key numbers: national wealth, international indebtedness, and assets and liabilities outstanding by sector (all data representing amounts at year's end)
Reporting agency and source publication: StatsCan, *National Balance Sheet Accounts*, #13-214-XPB; StatsCan *Daily*; StatsCan, *A Guide to the Financial Flow and National Balance Sheet Accounts*, #13-585E (excellent description of *NBSA*).
Website: www.statcan.ca
Usual timing: with *NIEA*
Reference period: previous quarter's end
Revisions: as *NIEA*

Description

The *NBSA* describes the non-financial assets owned in the sectors of the economy and of the financial claims outstanding among transactors in the economy. They consist of the balance sheets of all sectors. National wealth is the sum of non-financial, or tangible assets, produced assets, land surrounding structures, and agricultural land in all sectors. National net worth is wealth less what is owed to non-residents (Canada's net international investment position, or net foreign debt); alternatively, it is the sum of the net worth of persons, corporations, and governments.

National Economic and Financial Accounts (NEFA)

The NEFA incorporates two important components of the SNA: (I) **Financial Flow Accounts** and (II) **National Income and Expenditure Accounts**.

I: Financial Flow Accounts

Key numbers: financial market summary table (Table 1)
Reporting agency and source publication: StatsCan, *Financial Flow Accounts*, #13-014; StatsCan *Daily*; and StatsCan, *A Guide to the Financial Flow and National Balance Sheet Accounts*, #13-585E
Website: www.statcan.ca

Usual timing: with quarterly release of **NIEA**
Reference period: previous quarter
Survey period: entire quarter
Revisions: as for NIEA

II: National Income and Expenditure Accounts (NIEA)

Key numbers: real GDE and implicit GDE deflator, annualized percentage change from previous quarter
Reporting agency and source publication: StatsCan, *National Income and Expenditure Accounts*, #13-001-PPB; StatsCan *Daily*; StatsCan, *Guide to the Income and Expenditure Accounts*, #13-603E (an excellent lay account of **NIEA**)
Website: www.statcan.ca
Usual timing:
Reference period: previous quarter
Survey period: entire quarter
Revisions: year to date; four years with first quarter data

Quarterly Financial Statistics for Enterprises

Key numbers: income statements and balance sheet data for total of all industries and for individual industries
Reporting agency and source publications: StatsCan, *Quarterly Financial Statistics for Enterprises*, #61-008-XPB, StatsCan *Daily*
Website: www.statcan.ca
Usual timing: about fifty days after end of quarter
Reference period: latest quarter
Survey period: entire quarter
Revisions: previous quarter

Description

This publication provides data on twenty-two non-financial industries, eight financial industries, and their totals. For each industry, it offers three financial statements in a standard format: a balance sheet, an income statement, and a statement of changes in financial position. It provides selected items on a seasonally adjusted basis: operating revenue, operating profit, profit before extraordinary gains, and net profit. In addition, it presents certain ratios: return on capital employed, return on equity, profit margin, ratio of debt to equity, and the working-capital ratio.

Significance

This publication is the only source of detailed, standardized, aggregate balance-sheet data for Canadian industries, except for certain financial institutions, for which the quarterly *Bank of Canada Review* presents highly detailed data on assets and liabilities.

Limitations

StatsCan has recently rebuilt its register of Canadian businesses to try to improve the comprehensiveness of its survey of larger corporations and to reduce bias in its sampling of smaller firms. It samples 6,000 enterprises to ensure that the data are representative at the industry level. Given the existence of large conglomerates and holding companies within Canada's corporate sector, it will always be difficult to keep pace with mergers, acquisitions, and restructurings and to separate out the data into the appropriate industry categories. None the less, the data are both timely and useful.

ANNUAL INDICATORS

Environmental Indicators

StatsCan has begun to publish an annual compendium of environment-related statistics entitled *Econnections*, #16-200-XKE. The first release consists of a printed publication offering ten summary indicators and a CD-ROM database containing detailed supporting statistics. The ten indicators are: Natural Resource Wealth, Physical Quantities of Natural Resource Assets, Total Resource Base, Agricultural Land Use and Supply, Urban Land Use, Energy Use per Unit of Household Expenditure, Water Use per Unit of Household Expenditure, Greenhouse Gas Emissions per Unit of Household Expenditure, Environmental Protection Expenditures in the Business Sector, and Pollution Abatement and Control Expenditures in the Government Sector. *Econnections* results from a major, continuing effort to integrate environmental and economic statistics within the SNA framework, allowing measurement of the environment's contribution to economic well-being as well as the effects of economic activity on the environment. Prospective users should also acquire *Concepts, Sources and Methods of the Canadian System of Environmental and Resource Accounts*, #16-505-GPE.

12

The U.S. Indicators

A convenient way of obtaining data on the U.S. economy is through the website operated by the U.S. Department of Commerce: domino.stat-usa.gov/. Updated daily, it provides easy access to a large number of significant daily, weekly, monthly, and quarterly series. In addition, it carries speeches by Federal Reserve Board officials, the Economic Report of the President, and a schedule of the indicators' release dates. Some data can be accessed free; lengthier series are available by subscription (credit cards are accepted online).

A website that provides a huge number of links to sites of interest is entitled Resources for Economists on the Internet; it can be found at COBA.SHSU.edu/ EconFAQ/EconFAQ.html. Another good roundup with commentary on sources can be found at www.clark.net/pub/lschank/web/ecostats.html. A number of sources provide surveys of opinion about what the indicators will show: one such is www.briefing.com/Schwab/markcal.htm.

This chapter presents weekly, monthly, and quarterly U.S. indicators.

WEEKLY INDICATORS

Initial State Unemployment Insurance Claims

Key number: the level of initial UI claims (SA)
Reporting agency and source publication: Department of Labor, Employment and Training Administration, *Unemployment Insurance Weekly Claims Report*
Website: www.dol.gov/dol/public/media/main.htm
Usual timing: Thursday (8:30 a.m.)
Reference period: second week before release
Revisions: previous week

Description and Significance

Average Initial UI Claims form part of the (U.S.) Conference Board's Leading Indicator. Initial claims (that is, claims made by those who have just qualified for benefits) are widely watched in financial markets because they are thought to be helpful in forecasting changes in unemployment. Unfortunately, changes in initial claims are not strongly correlated with changes in unemployment or employment (either survey) in the same month, so they are not really a good predictor for this purpose.

MONTHLY INDICATORS

Capacity Utilization (Industry Operating Rate)

Key number: overall rate of capacity use for manufacturing, mining, and electric and gas utilities
Reporting agency and source publication: Federal Reserve Board, *Industrial Production and Capacity Utilization*, G17
Website: www.bog.frb.fed.us/releases/G17/
Usual timing: mid-month (9:15 a.m.); release dates provided in advance at website
Reference period: previous month
Revisions: two months back or more; data revised annually (sometimes significantly) to take account of new sources of information

Description and Significance

Rates of capacity use are an indication of the pressure of demand on the available supply in goods-producing industries and can thus help to clarify the inflation outlook in those sectors. However, there are many problems in interpreting the data, which are only a very rough guide in this context. Each industry has different operating characteristics: some get into serious bottlenecks at surprisingly low utilization rates; others appear to operate without much stress at over 100 per cent. Companies operate an ever-changing collection of machines and equipment of various ages and technologies – almost impossible to capture in a single number.

Normally, when industrial production rises, the rate of capacity use tends to increase at the same time. In fact the only real monthly information is in the production data; the utilization rate is simply calculated from it, since the amount of capital stock employed in an industry in the short run is essentially given. The website gives access to helpful methodological information.

Car Sales

Key numbers: unit sales of domestic and imported cars and light trucks
Reporting agency: Bureau of Economic Analysis (BEA)
Website: domino.stat-usa.gov/bea/gap-gtp.bea
Usual timing: first week of month (usually after 4:00 p.m.)
Reference period: previous month
Survey period: entire month
Revisions: usually none, but varies

Description

The tables provide unit data on unadjusted and seasonally adjusted auto and truck sales, domestic auto production (refers to autos assembled in the United States), Canadian and Mexican auto imports, auto exports, and domestic auto inventories.

Significance

New autos account for only a small proportion of consumer spending on goods (about 5 per cent), but it is their volatility that makes them important. They are sensitive to interest rates and incentive programs and may rise or fall sharply, with a large impact on real GDP growth. The BEA uses seasonally adjusted data on auto and truck sales and seasonally adjusted auto inventories in preparing esti-mates of personal consumption expenditures, producers' durable equipment, and changes in the business-inventories components of GDP, which are produc-ed by the BEA as part of the **National Income and Product Accounts** (NIPA).

Consumer Confidence Index

Key number: index level, change from previous month
Reporting agency and source publication: (U.S.) Conference Board
Website: www.crc-conquest.org/
Usual timing: last Tuesday of month
Reference period: current month
Revisions: none

Description

The index (1985 = 100) is based on a representative sample of 5,000 U.S. households. The board polls respondents on their views on employment, incomes, and business conditions generally, both currently and over the next six months. This index is a useful indicator of consumer sentiment, with some power to predict consumption behaviour.

Consumer Credit

Key number: net new consumer credit outstanding in $billion (SA), change in amount outstanding from previous month
Reporting agency and source publication: Federal Reserve Board (FRB), *Consumer Credit*, G19
Website: www.bog.frb.fed.us/releases/G19
Usual timing: fifth working day of month
Reference period: second month before release
Revisions: two months; annual revision affecting several years made in April

Significance

The increase in outstanding consumer credit is a useful measure of consumers' confidence in their capacity to carry debt. An increase in the rate of growth is strongly suggestive of further strength in consumer outlays in coming months – but it may also imply such a head of steam under spending as to encourage the FRB to increase short-term interest rates.

Limitations

Various forms of credit carry widely different financing charges. Many consumers regularly pay off their outstanding credit-card charges quickly enough to avoid paying interest; auto dealers and other merchandisers of durable goods regularly use cheap credit as a selling tool. A shift to extended credit terms can reduce monthly payments while increasing total interest costs over the life of a contract. For these and other reasons, the credit data must be interpreted with care.

Consumer Price Index (CPI)

Key numbers: CPI-U All Items (SA), percentage change from previous month and from previous year; also sub-indexes (as of January 1999): Food and Beverage, Housing, Apparel, Transportation, Medical Care, Recreation, Education and Communication, Energy, and All Items excluding Food and Energy
Reporting agency: Bureau of Labor Statistics (BLS), Department of Labor

Website: stats.bls.gov/cpihome.htm. Note: At stats.bls.gov/sahome.html, users can create their own retrieval list of BLS data, including CPI.
Usual timing: mid-month (8:30 a.m.)
Reference period: previous month
Survey period: three six-day periods during month
Revisions: none from one month to next; February, when January index released, seasonal factors for previous five years revised

Description

The CPI, a measure of the prices paid by urban consumers for a fixed basket of goods and services, is probably the most familiar of all measures of inflation. The U.S. CPI is constructed on the basis of a survey of consumer expenditure conducted approximately every ten years, most recently in 1993–5. This establishes a representative basket of goods and services, which is then priced by a survey during a pre-set six-day period each month. The CPI indexes prices relative to base-period levels (1982–4 until December 1998; 1993–5 thereafter) and then combines the resulting individual price indexes into a weighted arithmetic average to produce aggregate indexes for eight major commodity groups and for the all-items CPI. It subdivides the eight groups into classes and the classes into over 200 item strata; it surveys the item strata, represented by 'entry-level items,' each month in eighty-five urban areas. (Men's footwear is an item stratum within the footwear class within the apparel group; the specific footwear priced depends on what is found in stores each month.) The BLS publishes separate indexes for four regions and for a number of urban areas.

Though the weight of each item in the basket is fixed by the decennial survey, its relative contribution to the value of the CPI changes as its price rises or falls relative to the prices of other items.

The CPI-U versus the CPI-W

The CPI that represents the purchasing habits of urban consumers – the so-called CPI-U, for urban – is the best-known version, but a CPI-W, for wage, is published as well. The CPI-U is constructed to reflect the purchasing habits of the population at large, excluding rural, farm, military, and institutionalized individuals. The CPI-W is constructed to reflect the expenditure patterns of a narrower subset of urban consumers, namely those who earned more than half their income from clerical or wage occupations and who were employed for at least thirty-seven weeks in the last twelve months. This measure is often used for calculating wage payments due under collectively bargained cost-of-living-agreements.

The website provides access to much additional information.

Significance

The CPI is one of the most important indicators of inflation, since it represents the best available measure of changes in the purchasing power of a dollar in relation to a fixed basket of consumer goods and services. Some of the series in the CPI are used as inputs to the deflators for personal consumption expenditures in the calculation of GDE. Its timeliness (it appears within three weeks of the close of the month) enhances its value to financial-market participants.

Reliability and Limitations

The CPI has three characteristics that make it particularly valuable. It is timely, providing a detailed picture of developments in consumer prices until, on average, four to five weeks before the release. Its data are firm, in the sense that the BLS carries out a complete pre-set survey every month and provides complete information, making revisions unnecessary. And its information content is well established: where methodological problems exist (as with home ownership), intensive study over many years has established the virtues and limitations of alternative approaches.

In one major respect the CPI is potentially misleading. Because it is based on a fixed basket of items that is updated only once a decade, it takes little account of the changing buying habits of consumers between updates. Nor is there an adjustment between updates to reflect the availability of new items. The 'quality' of goods and services is monitored, however, and if an item becomes unavailable because of a model change, an upgrade, or seasonality, a new item or a later model replaces it in the index and its 'price' is adjusted downward to the extent that it is 'better' than the old one.

Partly because of the omission of 'new goods,' the U.S. CPI possibly overstates the increase in prices paid by households by some 1–2 per cent a year.[1] The deflator for personal consumption expenditure in the U.S. **NIPA**, which uses continuously updated weights, has fewer such problems. Sometimes the CPI rises faster than the deflator, and at other times more slowly; however, the two indexes behave quite similarly over long periods.

---

1   The Canadian CPI is thought to be less vulnerable to such concerns.

Differences from Canada's CPI

Most industrialized countries compute a CPI on similar principles. However, there are major differences in the weighting and coverage of the U.S. and Canadian CPIs, of which two deserve special note. In the United States, where a far greater proportion of the costs of medical care are borne by consumers, the CPI weights these costs more heavily. Also, Canada uses a measure based on replacement cost for homeowners' costs, which includes changes in house prices and mortgage rates – i.e., the costs of owning an asset. The U.S. measure of homeowners' costs treats them as equivalent to renters and prices only the implicit value of the shelter services that they consume.

Durable Goods Orders

Key numbers: total new orders for durable goods and its component non-defence capital goods: percentage change from previous month
Reporting agency and source publication: Bureau of the Census (BCN), Department of Commerce, *Advance Report on Durable Goods*
Website: www.census.gov/ftp/pub/indicator/www/m3/index.htm
Usual timing: advance release during last week of month following reference month (8:30 a.m.); full report during first week of second month after reference month (10:00 a.m.)
Reference period: previous month
Revisions: one month; also seasonal factor recomputed, affecting year-ago month; annual revision, usually affecting the most recent three years, in spring–summer, reflecting new benchmark data from annual survey of manufacturing or census

Description

The measure includes only orders placed with U.S. suppliers, not orders to foreign suppliers. It calculates new orders as follows: new orders equals current month's shipments plus current month's unfilled orders minus prior month's unfilled orders. Thus the estimate of new orders includes orders received and filled in the same month as well as orders not yet filled. It also includes the effects of cancellations and modifications of previously reported orders. The date for inclusion in orders is the date on which the company receives a firm (i.e., legally binding) order. This date may be considerably earlier than the date on which the order is made public.

Significance

Orders for non-defence capital goods correlate quite well with private-sector outlays on producers' durable equipment, tending to lead them a little in time as well. Thus the series is very helpful in forecasting spending on producers' durable equipment and helps to project manufacturing employment and industrial production as well.

Strong growth in orders may also indicate an improvement in the merchandise trade balance in subsequent months, either because of increased shipments abroad or because domestic producers are reducing imports by displacing foreign suppliers.

However, orders for non-defence capital goods are very volatile, and they are also subject to considerable revision. It is necessary to smooth them with moving averages of three months or more to get a reasonably reliable indicator of trend. Because some orders such as those for commercial aircraft are exceptionally large, BCN smooths them before publication – that is, distributes them over a number of months. Aircraft and space equipment have an especially long lead time; aircraft typically can take two and a half years to deliver. Therefore these orders may substantially precede the actual outlays in GDE.

Notes

The release of **Factory Orders** a week later, which reports orders for non-durable as well as for durable goods, revises the latter slightly with the benefit of more data. Other series that provide information about orders are Machine Tool Orders (National Association of Machine Tool Builders), Defense Department monthly procurement and applications, and the **Purchasing Managers' Survey** for the preceding month.

Employment and Unemployment

The Bureau of Labor Statistics (BLS) publishes two surveys each month in *The Employment Situation*, which I examine in parts I and II of this section. The BLS bases its survey of Payroll Employment (**Establishment Survey**) on payroll records from a sample of over 390,000 establishments, employing some 48 million people. It relates to the pay period including the twelfth of the month. It provides data on employment, hours worked, and hourly earnings of workers on non-farm payrolls. The BLS bases its **Household Survey**, in contrast, on a Bureau of the Census sample of about 50,000 households, which covers about a quarter of the labour force. It relates to the calendar week that includes the twelfth of the month. It provides data on the labour force, total employment, and unemployment. The sample rotates, so that in a given month 75 per cent of respondents are the same as in the previous month.

The payroll survey excludes agriculture, the self-employed, unpaid family workers, private household workers, and members of the resident armed forces. The household survey excludes those under sixteen years old. It counts an individual only once, while the payroll survey counts him or her separately for each job if he or she has more than one; roughly 5 per cent of workers are in this category. The household survey counts workers on strike as employed.

I: The Establishment Survey

Key numbers: change in total non-farm payroll employment from previous month, average hours worked per week, average hourly earnings, change in manufacturing employment
Reporting agency and source publication: Bureau of Labor Statistics, *The Employment Situation*
Website: stats.bls.gov:80/proghome.htm
Usual timing: first Friday of month after reference month (with Household Survey, 8:30 a.m.)
Reference period: pay period containing twelfth of month
Revisions: two months back; annual revision in early June, reflecting new benchmark data and revisions to seasonal factors for five years back

Description

This report is based on a survey of payrolls in the weekly pay period containing the twelfth of the month. The survey excludes agricultural workers, the self-employed, resident members of the armed forces, private household workers, and unpaid family workers and covers about 40 per cent of total employment. It does not count workers on strike as employed but includes government workers.

In the survey, 'employed' means that the person in question received pay for any part of the reference period. There is no age restriction, in contrast to the **Household Survey**, which measures only people sixteen years of age and over. The survey provides data on the number employed, average hours worked, and average hourly earnings at a substantially disaggregated industry level – for example, 'chemicals and allied products' within 'non-durable goods' within 'goods-producing industries.'

Significance

These data help in forecasting the **National Income and Product Accounts (NIPA)**. First, the NIPA uses employment by state and local governments in estimating state- and local-government spending on goods and services. Second, it derives the wage and salary component of personal income from employment multiplied by hours worked multiplied by average hourly earnings. Third, the NIPA estimates consumption of services such as medical care, education, and financial services from employment in those industries multiplied by hours worked multiplied by hourly earnings.

Employment in goods-producing industries typically varies considerably more over a business cycle than that in service industries. The twelve-month rate of change of employment is a good indicator of the shifting fortunes of key industries such as manufacturing, construction, and the retail sector. Once a trend has established itself, it tends to persist. Note, however, that peaks and troughs in the level of employment lag behind those in the level of output.

The monthly data on average hourly earnings provide the earliest indications of wage inflation trends, though the quarterly **Employment Cost Index** contains much more information on labour compensation as a whole.

Multiplying average hours worked by average hourly earnings by employment gives an early indication of trends in labour income.

Reliability and Limitations

The financial markets pay great attention to monthly changes in non-farm payrolls, the sizes of which are typically subject to significant revisions in each of the following two months. However, the amount of revision to the total number of people employed – typically about 0.06 per cent between the original estimate and the second revision – is respectably low. As well, since months differ in length, the increase will tend to be larger in long months than in short months. The survey makes no adjustment for this fact. Fortunately, it is unusual for hours worked and average hourly earnings to be significantly revised after the original estimates are released.

II: The Household Survey

Key numbers: civilian unemployment rate, number of employed persons, size of labour force, working-age population, rate of participation in labour force
Reporting agency and source publication: Bureau of Labor Statistics (BLS), *The Employment Situation*

Website: stats.bls.gov:80/proghome.htm
Usual timing: first Friday of month following reference week (8:30 a.m.)
Reference period: calendar week including twelfth of month
Survey period: week following reference week
Revisions: none on a month-to-month basis; annual revision with December release (in January), with seasonal factors revised for five years back

Description

The 'unemployed' are those who did not work but were available and searched for work sometime during the preceding four weeks, workers who were laid off and are waiting to be recalled, and persons waiting to start a new job in thirty days or less. All sampled persons who worked for one hour or more in the week are counted as employed.

The 'employed' include members of the resident armed forces. However, the unemployment rate reported is the 'civilian unemployment rate,' measured as unemployment divided by the civilian labour force only.

Significance

The Household Survey provides a great deal of detail on the age, sex, race, industry, and occupation of the employed. The number of self-employed persons can be used to estimate unincorporated business income. The ratio of civilian employment to the working-age population is a very important guide to the state of consumer confidence. Information about part-time work, and about the length of unemployment spells, gives an indication of the tightness of labour-market conditions and thus of wage-rate prospects. The survey also indicates which part-time work is voluntary and which is not: the changing ratio of voluntary to involuntary part-time work is a useful, sensitive indicator of labour-market conditions.

Factory Orders

Key numbers: manufacturers' new orders (percentage change from previous month)
Reporting agency and source publication: Bureau of the Census, *Manufacturers' Shipments, Inventories, and Orders*
Website: www.census.gov/ftp/pub/indicator/www/m3/index.htm
Usual timing: early in month (10:00 a.m.)
Reference period: second month before release

Revisions: one month and concurrently a revision to seasonal adjustment for a year ago as well; for annual revision, **Durable Goods Orders**

Description

Released a week after Durable Goods Orders, this updates them and includes orders for non-durable goods as well. The release contains an aggregate series for durable goods and two special groupings: non-defence capital goods, which includes goods ordered by NASA, and defence capital goods. The data on orders include goods purchased by both domestic and foreign companies but not goods purchased by U.S. buyers from foreign suppliers.

The estimate of new orders is derived from the monthly estimate of ship-ments plus the change in unfilled orders between the current and prior period. The estimate includes orders received and filled in the same month as well as those not yet filled. It also includes the effects of cancellations and modifica-tions of previously reported orders.

Reliability and Limitations

Revisions to the advance report are often substantial in subsequent months. Since the financial markets often react strongly to the report, it is useful to remember this shortcoming. Even after revision, month-to-month change is typically quite volatile, so it is probably useful to calculate a moving average of three months or so and watch its rate of change over a longer period.

Federal Government Budget Balance

Reporting agency and source publication: U.S. Department of Treasury, *Monthly Treasury Statement of Receipts and Outlays of the Government.* The website contains links to a number of useful publications, including the U.S. Budget, the monthly statement of the U.S. Public Debt, the Economic Report of the President, and discussions of the fiscal outlook by the Congressional Budget Office.
Website: www.fms.treas.gov/mts/index.html
Usual timing: fifteenth business day of month
Reference period: previous month
Survey period: entire month
Revisions: usually none

Help-Wanted Index

Key numbers: index and percentage change from previous month
Reporting agency: U.S. Conference Board
Website: www.conference-board.org
Usual timing: last Thursday of month (10:00 a.m.)
Reference period: month before release
Revisions: usually none

Description

The Help-Wanted Index is an indicator of job availability and is often used as a leading indicator of economic activity. Turning points in the index have typically preceded those in output by three to seven months. The board compiles each city index by surveying one major newspaper in each of fifty-one standard metropolitan statistical areas (SMSAs) for want-ad volume and adjusting the results for the length of the month and for seasonality. It compiles regional and national indexes from these data by weighting city indexes according to non-agricultural employment in each city and summing the weighted indexes.

Reliability and Significance

Turning points in the Help-Wanted Index correspond to changes in the unemployment rate – an increase in the index is associated with a decrease in unemployment. Changes in the index lead changes in the unemployment rate by about three months. Unfortunately, since both measures tend to fluctuate before turning definitely in one direction, and since the index is reported a month after the corresponding month's unemployment rate, it is not a very useful predictor. The index also tends to be quite volatile from month to month – its percentage declines have historically been three to four times as large as declines in industrial production.

Other factors also make the index unreliable. When data are unavailable for a city, estimates are made based on the regional index for the unavailable city, or the national index if more than one city in a region is missing. In addition, the index may not measure accurately the availability of unskilled jobs in a city or region, since want ads are placed primarily to attract professionals and skilled labour.

Household Survey

See **Employment and Unemployment**, part II, above.

Housing Starts

Key numbers: total starts and building permits (SAAR)
Reporting agency and source publication: Bureau of the Census (BCN),
Construction Report, *Housing Starts*, Series C20
Website: domino.stat-usa.gov/cen/house.cen
Usual timing: mid-month (8:30 a.m.)
Reference period: previous month
Revisions: two months back; each February, seasonal factors revised for three
years back

Description

The BCN divides housing starts into single units, two to four units, and five
units and up. It counts a 'start' when excavation for footings or the foundation
has begun. Thus when an apartment building is started, it counts the total
number of units in the building at once. It does not include mobile homes,
hotels, rooming-houses, student accommodation, and conversions in starts.

Significance

The **NIPA** uses the number of starts and the cost of construction taken from
the building-permits survey to estimate the new-housing component of
residential construction. And, of course, since new homes must be furnished,
there is a predictable, lagged impact on the demand for consumer durable
goods such as furniture. Housing starts are widely watched because, like auto
sales, they are an early, sensitive indicator of consumers' willingness to spend.
But the monthly data are not as useful in forecasting the economy as is sometimes suggested. They are subject to quite erratic swings, and it is usually
necessary to have three months of data to determine a change in direction.
Some of this volatility can be attributed to weather. Once a trend has emerged,
however, it tends to persist. Though residential construction and household
durable expenditures do not account for much of GDE, the size of their swings
gives them extra weight in determining the direction of the economy as a
whole.

Reliability and Limitations

Multi-unit starts can be especially volatile from month to month, because a given start can add a huge number of units.

One might expect housing permits to be a good indicator of the next month's starts, but they are not. Most of the units for which a permit is granted are actually started in the same month. In any case, a permit merely indicates an intention to build. About 2 per cent of permits are never translated into starts, and about 2 per cent of starts do not obtain a permit.

Index of Industrial Production

Key numbers: index of industrial production (SA), percentage change from previous month
Reporting agency and source publication: Federal Reserve Board, *Industrial Production and Capacity Utilization*, G17
Website: www.bog.frb.fed.us/releases/G17/
Usual timing: mid-month (9:15 a.m.), release dates published on website in advance
Reference period: previous month
Revisions: three months; annual revision in December

Description

This index (1992 = 100) measures the output of the manufacturing, mining, and gas and electric utility industries. It excludes farms and the construction, transportation, trade, and service industries but includes production at government-owned factories. There is a great deal of detailed information on individual industries. See also **Capacity Utilization**.

Since the level of industrial production is roughly coincident in time with GDP as a whole, the report is less useful for projecting changes in direction than for the volume of detail it provides on individual industries.

Underlying surveys and methods are discussed on the website.

Index of Leading Indicators

Key numbers: Index of leading indicators (SA), percentage change from previous month
Reporting agency and source publication: U.S. Conference Board

Website: www.tcb-indicators.org
Usual timing: first week of month (10:00 a.m.)
Reference period: second month before release
Revisions: may go back many months and can be quite large

Description

Series included in the Index of Leading Indicators are Average Manufacturing Workweek (hours); Average Weekly Initial Claims for State Unemployment Insurance (thousands); New Orders in Consumer Goods and Materials Industries (1992 $million); Vendor Performance (a diffusion index of delivery lags, percentage); Orders for Non-defense Capital Goods (1992 $million); Building Permits (thousands); Stock Prices (S&P 500 Index, 1941–43 = 10); M-2 (1992 $billion); Interest Rate Spread, 10-year Treasury Bonds less Federal Funds; Index of Consumer Expectations (University of Michigan survey, 1966:1 = 100).

A description of method and other information is available at the website.

Significance

The percentage change in the Leading Index from the previous month is the most important statistic in the release. The idea is that the index provides a good indication of the strength of the economy and predicts turning points in GDE, by weighting together indicators from many different sectors, each of which tends to turn sooner than GDE itself.

Reliability and Limitations

By the time it is released, there is very little surprise left in the Leading Index, because most of the components are already known. The components in the three indexes — Leading, Coincident, and Lagging — were chosen because of their past behaviour relative to GDE. Some forecasters also believe that the ratio of the Coincident Index to the Lagging Index is a useful forecasting tool. But financial-market participants already follow many different indicators very closely. To reduce a set of indicators to one number actually throws away known information. None the less, financial markets do often respond visibly to the release.

A number of the components in the indexes are subject to significant revision, so the revision of the indexes themselves can give markedly different readings from the initial release.

International Trade

Key numbers: exports and imports (SA) and the difference between them; balances with Japan, Canada, western Europe, and OPEC; balances for particular commodity groups; imports of crude petroleum.

Reporting agencies and source publication: Bureau of the Census and Bureau of Economic Analysis (Department of Commerce), *U.S. International Trade in Goods and Services*, FT900

Website: www.census.gov/foreign-trade/www/press.html

Usual timing: mid-month (8:30 a.m.)

Reference period: second month before release (delay imposed to ensure that shipments that actually entered or left ports in a given month are as much as possible included in release, but reporting lags so long that some 2 to 4 per cent of shipments still not picked up until following month)

Revisions: for goods, one month, usually fairly modest in scope; in May, with release of March data, one year of history revised; for services, one month, with no further changes until release of quarterly estimates of international transactions, based on more complete data; first monthly release following quarterly estimates to contain revised estimates for previous six months; annual revision in May, as for goods

Description

Trade in goods is reported both on a Census basis and a Balance of Payments (BOP) basis. The former system reports goods exports on an FAS basis ('free aboard ship' – that is, including all costs incurred up to the dockside, including inland freight and insurance), while imports of goods do not include costs of insurance and freight incurred to bring goods to the U.S. border. Data for U.S. exports to Canada are derived from import data compiled by Canada, adjusted to remove goods from third countries imported through the United States and to include inland freight charges. For BOP reporting, small adjustments are made to export data to standardize them with SNA practice; imports are valued at the foreign port of export.

Services, shown in seven broad categories, are based on quarterly, annual, and benchmark surveys and partial information generated from monthly reports. No country or area detail is available on a monthly basis because source data are lacking.

Significance

U.S. trade in merchandise (goods) has been increasingly important in recent years. A country's merchandise exports will tend to increase quickly either when foreign economies are growing rapidly or when domestic demand is growing relatively slowly. Similarly, merchandise imports tend to increase rapidly when domestic demand overpresses home capacity or when foreign economies are underused. Because the United States grew faster than its trading partners in the early and mid-1990s, its merchandise deficit has worsened, exacerbated by the relatively tight monetary stance of the Federal Reserve Board, which helped to bring about a real appreciation of the U.S. dollar, making U.S. goods appear increasingly expensive to foreigners and foreign goods cheap to U.S. residents.

As a net lender, the United States has over the years generated a substantial net inflow of investment income from foreigners, especially in the form of interest payments, and this situation has continued, but it has been eroded by a growing flow of interest outpayments. A trade deficit is not all bad. It reduces inflationary pressures by siphoning excess demand off to other countries. When a central bank tightens monetary policy, with the effect of raising the real exchange rate, the resulting deterioration of the trade balance is part of the 'treatment.' However, if all the major trading partners are overheated at the same time, so that it is no longer possible to shift demand towards a partner with underused capacity, then all must restrain themselves if inflation is to be brought down.

Fiscal restraint, conversely, tends to depress interest rates and the exchange rate (because it reduces the private sector's need to borrow from abroad) and thus is relatively supportive to the trade balance as well as to interest-sensitive outlays such as investment, while depressing income-sensitive outlays such as consumption. This is a major reason why a forecaster, in projecting the contribution of various sectors to the outlook, will need to make a careful assessment of the mix of monetary and fiscal measures likely to be adopted.

Money Supply

Key numbers: currency in circulation, M1, and M2 (all SA)
Reporting agency and source publication: Federal Reserve Board (FRB), *Money Stock, Liquid Assets and Debt Measures*, H.6
Website: www.bog.frb.fed.us/releases/H6/
Usual timing: Thursday afternoons at 4:30 p.m.
Reference period: previous month
Revisions: usually very small, for previous month; seasonal factors for past years recalculated and released in early February

Description

The H.6 release provides data on the monetary aggregates (M1, M2, and M3), a broad measure of liquidity (L), and domestic non-financial debt and on their components. M1 is money narrowly defined, consisting of the most liquid financial items – currency and chequable deposits. (Outstanding travellers' cheques are counted as money in M1 in the United States, but not in Canada.) M2 and M3 are broader monetary aggregates. M2 includes M1 and what are primarily household holdings of savings deposits, time deposits, and retail money-market mutual funds. M3 includes M2 along with institutional money funds and certain managed liabilities of depositories (large time deposits, repurchase agreements, and Eurodollars).

We usually think of 'money' as liquid (quickly exchangeable for something else without significant loss), but some time deposits included in M2 and M3 are not actually very liquid, because they may not be cashable before maturity or be cashable only at a penalty.

The Canadian and U.S. definitions of money differ significantly. The names M1, M2, and M3 represent different aggregations of assets in each country, though their general meaning is similar. In both countries, M1 includes assets that are held primarily to facilitate spending. M2 and M3 are successively broader aggregates, including assets also held for other purposes: to reduce portfolio risk and to earn interest. In the United States, all chequable deposits are included in M1 even if they pay interest, but in Canada interest-bearing deposits are excluded from M1. U.S. M2 includes some money-market-fund balances; in Canada, these are part of M2 plus. U.S. M2 and M3 both include deposits at non-bank 'thrift' institutions such as savings and loan associations (S&Ls), but Canadian M2 and M3 do not. Compare the notes to Table 1 of this release with Table 8 in this volume.

The FRB also publishes an even broader measure of liquidity than M3, which it calls 'L.' This consists of M3 plus holdings by the non-bank public of U.S. Savings Bonds, short-term Treasury securities, commercial paper and bankers' acceptances, net of money-market-fund holdings of these assets, already measured in M3.

Differences in Function between Types of Deposits

Types of deposits differ in function. For example, the average U.S. demand deposit does not pay interest; it is held typically as a working cash balance by companies and on average is 'turned over' about six hundred times a year (that is, the volume of cheques written in a year is roughly six hundred times the average balance). Demand deposits at major New York City banks turn over

2,700 times a year! This reflects the banking requirements of the securities industry. If these banks are excluded, average turnover in demand deposits falls to about 350 times per year. Other chequable deposits, which pay interest and are held largely by individuals, turn over on average only about fourteen times a year. For money-market deposit accounts, turnover is roughly five times a year, and for savings deposits, about three.

Demand deposits, which do not pay interest, are held almost solely to facilitate payments. Other deposits, while they can be and are used for making payments, are an important store of value, held in part to reduce the riskiness of the owner's overall portfolio – that is, the chance that he or she will be embarrassed by an unexpected event. Raising the interest rate paid on deposits will lead individuals to increase their holdings of them, at the expense of other assets whose expected yields have not risen.

Residents of many other countries make a practice of holding significant portions of their wealth in deposits with U.S. banks or even in the form of U.S. currency, as a result of chaotic political and monetary conditions at home. Participants in the U.S. underground economy probably hold large amounts of their wealth in the form of currency in order to keep it undetected by the authorities. There is no reliable estimate of the amount of such holdings.

Signals of U.S. Monetary Policy

The United States is divided into twelve Federal Reserve Districts, each with its own Federal Reserve Bank. The twelve banks are united in managing the Federal Reserve System (the 'Fed'), whose board of governors operates monetary policy through the Fed's Open Market Committee (FOMC). The chairman of the board (currently Alan Greenspan) is appointed by the president of the United States for a seven-year term. The Fed is required by legislation (the Humphrey–Hawkins Act) to report twice a year to Congress on its monetary policy and specifically to set targets for the growth of the major monetary aggregates in the coming year. In managing the monetary aggregates, the Federal Reserve Bank of New York, acting as the agent of the FOMC, continually adjusts the supply of settlement balances ('Federal Funds') available to the member commercial banks in the system, in such a way as to lead them to bid higher or lower among themselves for spare balances. The resulting changes in the 'Fed Funds rate' are quickly reflected in other short-term interest rates. From time to time, the Fed augments signals from the Fed Funds rate by moving its discount rate, which has little operational significance but can be counted on to get front-page coverage in the media.

Personal Income

Key numbers: personal income and consumption (SA), percentage change from previous month; the personal saving rate
Reporting agency and source publication: Bureau of Economic Analysis, *Personal Income and Outlays*
Website: domino.stat-usa.gov/bea/pi.bea
Usual timing: fourth week of month following reference month, or first week of month after that (8:30 a.m.)
Reference period: first or second month prior to release
Revisions: four months; annual revision in July or August, part of annual revision of **NIPA**, reflecting calculation of revised seasonal factors for three years of history as well as incorporation of more complete sources of data

Description

Personal income is the sum of wage and salary disbursements, proprietors' income (farm and non-farm), rental income, dividend income, interest income, and transfers to persons. When one subtracts social-insurance contributions and personal taxes, the remainder is personal disposable income (PDI). In turn, personal saving is defined as the residual after subtraction of consumption, interest payments, and transfers to non-residents from PDI. The personal saving rate is personal saving as a percentage of PDI.

Significance

Financial markets pay great attention to this monthly release, which provides the first detailed, comprehensive look at consumers' spending power and how they have managed it. Data on retail sales are released earlier in the month, but they provide no information on spending on services. In general, individuals manage their consumption in relation to their perception of sustainable income, so windfalls, such as special bonuses, tend largely to be saved at the time they are received. Conversely, when income is temporarily depressed – for instance, by layoffs – consumption tends to be maintained closer to its accustomed rate for a time. But the consumption of lower-income individuals and families, who have a lower capacity to save than those with higher incomes, tends to mirror very closely their actual receipts from month to month. Individuals' saving behaviour is influenced by age, family considerations, interest rates, and many other portfolio-managing concerns.

Personal income, consumption, and saving, which are estimated monthly in the United States, are estimated quarterly by Statistics Canada. The latter does estimate retail sales every month, but, as in the United States, only consumers' purchases of goods, not services.

A Note on Revisions

Data on monthly income and consumption are subject to (usually) modest revisions in the first few months after their initial release. Changes at the annual revision can be substantial, since they are based on more detailed and complete sources.

Producer Price Index (PPI)

Key numbers: PPI for Finished Goods, Intermediate Goods, and Crude Goods, and Finished Goods Excluding Food and Energy, percentage change from previous month (all SA)
Reporting agency and source publication: Bureau of Labor Statistics, *Producer Price Index*
Website: stats.bls.gov/ppihome.htm
Usual timing: second Friday of month, 8:30 a.m.; release dates published on website for coming year
Reference period: previous month
Revisions: with current month's release, fourth previous month revised, based on late reports and corrections by respondents; January revisions, usually minor, to seasonal factors for five years of seasonally adjusted data

Description

(U.S.) PPIs (the Canadian equivalent is the **Industrial Product Price Index**) are calculated from the selling prices of manufactured goods. Three basic indexes are compiled, for Finished Goods, Intermediate Goods, and Crude Goods. Each of these in turn is composed of a more detailed group of commodity indexes. Crude goods, as the name implies, are earliest in the chain of production, and their prices tend to move earlier (and often much more dramatically) than those for intermediate or finished goods. Because they are early, they can give helpful warning of future increases in consumer prices. But there are a number of reasons why CPIs do not simply reflect producer prices with a lag. The prices of crude goods tend to be very sensitive to transitory shifts in supply or demand pressures, which may be quickly reversed. Those who purchase them as inputs to production can and do anticipate such reverses and time their purchases accordingly. They also purchase in forward as well as spot markets to provide themselves with relative stability in their average input prices. As one moves further along the chain, the influence of cost pressures in transportation and distribution networks is added in, but even prices for 'finished goods' do not include the influence of changing wholesale and retail markups. And, of course, the prices of services to consumers, which account for more than half of U.S. consumer spending, are not included here at all.

Limitations

Month-to-month changes in the indexes are relatively volatile and thus are unreliable indicators of inflationary pressure. Since food prices tend to be heavily influenced by supply-side factors such as weather even over longer periods, and energy prices have been dominated in recent years by the special case of crude oil, financial markets have tended to place particular weight on the PPI for Finished Goods, Excluding Food and Energy in assessing inflationary trends. However, even its fluctuations are volatile enough to require care in interpretation.

Purchasing Managers' Survey

Key numbers: percentage of purchasing managers reporting an expected increase in production and employment
Reporting agency and source publication: National Association of Purchasing Managers, press release in the *Wall Street Journal*
Website: www.napm.org/public/rob/index2.html
Usual timing: turn of month, 10:00 a.m.
Reference period: month just ended
Revisions: none

Description

The association bases this composite index on a survey of its members about five major categories of activity: new orders, production, vendor deliveries, inventories, and employment. It compiles the survey from the responses of purchasing executives in over 300 industrial companies, who are asked to indicate the change if any from the previous month in each category (i.e., whether new orders were better or worse, or vendor deliveries were slower or faster). It then weights the seasonally adjusted data to form the overall index. A reading of 50 per cent or higher is considered to indicate that the economy is generally expanding; below 50 per cent indicates a recession. The distance from 50 per cent indicates the relative strength of the expansion or decline. Prices paid and the speed or slowness of vendor deliveries are widely followed as indicators of inflationary pressure.

Significance

As the survey for the previous month is released on the first business day of the next month, its timeliness makes it a widely followed indicator of changes in economic activity. The survey of the Chicago region is usually released a day or so earlier than the national average, and financial markets react strongly to it, especially to the data on orders. (The Federal Reserve Bank of Philadelphia releases a monthly survey of manufacturing even earlier, during the third week of the reference month.)

Retail Sales

Key numbers: total retail sales, retail sales ex auto dealers, durable goods, non-durable goods, percentage change from previous month and year earlier (all SA)
Reporting agency and source publications: Bureau of the Census (BCN), *Advance Monthly Retail Sales, Monthly Retail Sales and Inventories*
Website: www.census.gov/econ/www/retmenu.html
Usual timing: 'advance' estimates, based on a subsample of about 4,100 firms, released about nine working days after close of reference month (8:30 a.m.); data from full sample of 13,300 retail businesses released about six weeks after close of reference month; release dates published in December for following year
Reference period: previous month
Revisions: advance release with 'preliminary' data from full sample for previous month; full-sample release with preliminary data for reference month and final figures for prior twelve months; annual revision in March, with data for previous calendar year revised to reflect results from annual retail trade survey

Description

This release reports the sales and receipts of establishments engaged primarily in retail trade and excludes retail sales by manufacturers, wholesalers, and service establishments. 'Sales' include receipts for rentals and leases, delivery, repairs, maintenance, alterations, storage, and excise taxes paid by manufacturers, but the value of rebates and returns at the retail level is subtracted, as well as trade-in allowances, manufacturers' rebates, and the value of sales and excise taxes collected directly from customers.

Significance

Data on retail sales are the first comprehensive indication of consumers' purchases of goods for the month. The major limitation of the data is that they do not measure consumption of services – the largest part of U.S. consumer spending. However, consumption of services tends to stick close to its trend, whereas durables are volatile and tend to dominate the consumer cycle: for this reason, the retail sales release gets a lot of attention in financial markets. BCN uses retail sales excluding auto and gasoline sales as a direct input to the calculation of personal consumption on goods.

Limitations

The kind-of-business classification is not a very accurate indication of the sales of particular commodities, since the outlets are classified according to their primary source of receipts. For example, many food stores make substantial sales of non-food products, which none the less are reported under the heading of food. A similar caution applies to the interpretation of auto dealers' sales. It might appear natural to project this category from the earlier-released data on unit car sales, but auto dealers sell trucks, used cars, boats and trailers, and parts and repairs in addition to new cars. The auto-dealer category also includes auto- and home-supply stores. In any case, even the relationship between the monthly data on unit car sales and the estimate of the value of new car sales is quite loose: 'unit car sales' includes sales by the manufacturers to leasing companies or to government, which are excluded from the retail sample; the number of units sold ignores the model, therefore the value, mix of the total sales; retail rebates can cause large swings in the average receipts from month to month; and changes in exchange rates can affect the value of sales of imported cars. Thus an increase in unit car sales and a decline in auto dealers' receipts may well be reported in the same month.

A Note on Revisions

Because the advance estimates are based on a subsample of establishments, revisions in the month-to-month rate of change of sales are often large. As well, about 20 per cent of sales are typically not reported in time for inclusion.

QUARTERLY INDICATORS

Employment Cost Index (ECI)

Key numbers: index of total compensation (SA), percentage change from year earlier
Reporting agency and source publication: Bureau of Labor Statistics (BLS), *Employment Cost Index*
Website: stats.bls.gov:80/ecthome.htm
Usual timing: final week of first month in quarter
Reference period: previous quarter
Survey period: pay period including twelfth of last month in quarter
Revisions: none

Description

The ECI measures changes in the cost of labour, defined as total compensation per employee-hour worked. Its coverage is extensive, using a sample of about 17,000 occupations within some 5,100 establishments to represent the entire civilian non-farm population, excluding private households and the federal government. As the ECI is meant to measure employees' compensation, it does not include the self-employed. Roughly three-quarters of the index is accounted for by 'earnings,' including production bonuses, commissions, and cost-of-living allowances but excluding tips, non-production-related bonuses, and room and board. 'Benefits,' which make up the other quarter, include paid leave, supplemental pay (such as overtime), insurance benefits (such as life and dental insurance), pension and savings plans, legally required benefits (such as social security and unemployment insurance), and other benefits (such as severance pay).

Significance

The ECI gives the same weight to each category of workers each quarter, so it is not affected by changes in the composition of the labour force over time. The BLS elaborately disaggregates the data by industry and by type of work, so they provide an extremely sensitive and accurate indication of compensation trends, useful not only to policy-makers such as the Federal Reserve Board but also to those involved in setting compensation practices.

Note

The BLS intends to replace the ECI and other compensation and benefits surveys with a new National Compensation Survey, starting in 2000. See the website for further information.

National Income and Product Accounts (NIPA)

Key numbers: annualized percentage change in GDE at constant prices and its major components, and the price indexes for GDP and gross domestic purchases (all SAAR); fixed-weight GDE deflator also widely followed in financial markets

Reporting agency and source publication: Bureau of Economic Analysis (BEA), *Gross Domestic Product*

Website: domino.stat-usa.gov/bea/gdp.bea

Usual timing: advance release at end of first month following quarter; preliminary release at end of second month; final revision a month later

Reference period: previous quarter

Revisions: once a year in July or August, benchmark revisions going back five years or more

Description

The NIPA (the U.S. equivalent of Canada's **NIEA**) summarizes flows of final expenditure and income on a quarterly and annual basis. The discussion of the Canadian *NIEA* in chapter 1 largely applies to the NIPA as well, though with differences in detail. See also (U.S.) **Personal Income**.

The reliability of the advance release suffers from its having only two months' data on merchandise trade to work with; estimates of inventory accumulation, too, are typically subject to substantial revision between advance and preliminary releases. Normally, changes between the preliminary and final releases are much smaller.

Calculation of Prices and Quantities in U.S. GDP

Except for the most recent period, the annual and quarterly changes used to compute U.S. real GDP and prices are 'chain-type' measures based on a 'Fisher ideal' formula that incorporates weights from two adjacent years. For example, the 1992–3 percentage change in real GDP uses prices for 1992 and 1993 as weights, and the 1992–3 percentage change in price uses quantities for 1992 and 1993 as weights. Because the quantity and price-index numbers calculated in this way are symmetric, the product of the annual change in real GDP and the annual change in prices equals the annual change in current-dollar GDP.

In the most recent period, the BEA uses a variant of the standard quarterly formula because only one year's information is available for computing the index number weights. For this period, the BEA uses weights from two adjacent quarters to calculate the change from the preceding quarter. It also publishes a second measure of the price level, known as the 'implicit price deflator,' or the ratio of current-dollar value to the corresponding chained-dollar value multiplied by 100. Its values are very similar to those of the 'chain-type' price index.

As noted above in chapter 1, the Canadian *NIEA*'s primary presentation of real GDP uses current-period volume weights, but Statistics Canada also provides chain-type volume indexes and both chain- and fixed-weighted price indexes in the standard *NIEA* tables.

PRINTED IN U.S.A.   CAT. NO. 24 16